W9-CUQ-703

THE
SHOPPER
ECONOMY

THE
SHOPPER
ECONOMY

THE NEW WAY TO
ACHIEVE MARKETPLACE SUCCESS
BY TURNING BEHAVIOR INTO CURRENCY

LIZ CRAWFORD

New York   Chicago   San Francisco   Lisbon   London   Madrid   Mexico City
Milan   New Delhi   San Juan   Seoul   Singapore   Sydney   Toronto

The McGraw-Hill Companies

Copyright ©2012 by Liz Crawford. All rights reserved. Printed in the United States of America. Except as permitted under the United States Copyright Act of 1976, no part of this publication may be reproduced or distributed in any form or by any means, or stored in a data base or retrieval system, without the prior written permission of the publisher.

1 2 3 4 5 6 7 8 9 0 DOC/DOC 1 8 7 6 5 4 3 2

ISBN: 978-0-07-178717-8
MHID: 0-07-178717-8

e-book ISBN: 978-0-07-178718-5
e-book MHID: 0-07-178718-6

McGraw-Hill books are available at special quantity discounts to use as premiums and sales promotions, or for use in corporate training programs. To contact a representative, please e-mail us at bulksales@mcgraw-hill.com.

Library of Congress Cataloging-in-Publication Data
Crawford, Liz.
   The shopper economy : the new way to achieve marketplace success by turning behavior into currency / by Liz Crawford.
      p. cm.
   ISBN 978-0-07-178717-8 (alk. paper) — ISBN 0-07-178717-8 (alk. paper)
   1. Consumer behavior. 2. Customer loyalty. 3. Internet marketing. I. Title.
   HF5415.32.C735 2012
   658.8'342—dc23   2012000524

This book is printed on acid-free paper.

For Marcia and John Hoover

Contents

Acknowledgments

I would like to thank my editor at McGraw-Hill, Donya Dickerson, who set this book in motion by reaching out to me.

I am very grateful to the thought leaders in the industry who took the time to share their insights and expertise: John Andrews, Evan Brody, Amy Callahan, Joe Ciarello, Dan Frechtling, Bill Hanifin, Peter Hoyt, Jeff Johnson, Chris Keating, Michael Lazerow, Larry Lieberman, Wendy Liebmann, Ken Nisch and his able colleague Marcy Goldstein, Catherine Roe, Cyriac Roeding, Phil Rubin, Ted Rubin, Keith Simmons, Walker Smith, and Jeff Weidauer.

A special thanks goes to the boots-on-the-ground shoppers Sonia K., Tom M., Beth J., and Amy B., who shared candidly, and also to all of the experienced bloggers from Collective Bias.

I would also like to thank those at MARS Advertising who have given me so much kind encouragement, especially comrades-in-arms Tim Scholler and Kristen Buss, and also kind supporters Mary Tarczynski, Mark Jacobs, and John Panourgoius. Former Martians Nick Stoyanoff and Anne Howe shared savvy comments that furthered my thinking. I would like to thank Rob Rivenburgh for being a great listener and coach, and Ken Barnett, who inspired me with his gutsy approach to living.

Special acknowledgments go to Peter Hoyt, the effervescent and visionary founder of the Path to Purchase Institute, who has given me opportunities to stage my ideas, and to Al McClain, a steady supporter and wise head, who invited me into the impressive BrainTrust panel at RetailWire. I am also grateful to Tim Manners, who first published *The Shopper Economy* in the *Hub* and who has taken the time to hear my ramblings.

I would like to thank Jana Branch, who has been an invaluable sounding board from the moment we met. Special shout-outs go to Alan Gellman, who has challenged my thinking and set a high bar for rigorous analysis, and to Ramin Ganeshram, who has kept me well fed with encouragement, laughs, and seasoned advice. Thanks go to the indefatigable and savvy PR guru, Julie Whitney. A big thank you goes to Linda Janssen, the smartest marketer I know and a very dear friend.

A debt of gratitude goes to Vicki Madden, my fellow traveler and brainy friend, who shares a life of the mind, and my homies Barb and Max March, Alan Fletcher, and the gang on Long Lots. Thank you to Cali James, my inspiring and intrepid sister from another mother.

I would like to acknowledge my extended family, Judy Crawford and the whole Crawford family, the Yahnes, the Lavanishes, the Hooks, and the formidable Mahoney clan. Special thanks to Nick and Chris Mahoney Jr., who have brought fun, laughter, and a new perspective into my life.

I am grateful to my amazing and loving parents, Marcia and John Hoover, who always managed to provide both a springboard and a safety net so that I could shoot for the moon. Finally, this book would not have been possible without Chris Mahoney, whose love lets me thrive.

Foreword

In the fall of 2010, Liz Crawford e-mailed me a white paper she had written about the changes in shopping behavior brought about by the rapidly emerging digital universe. Smartphones, apps, tablets, and the Internet itself—things were exploding in new and often unexpected ways. Smart marketers were scrambling to absorb what was happening and apply what they were learning as quickly and effectively as possible. Liz was working at one of America's top shopper marketing agencies at the time, and her white paper was destined for the November edition of the *Hub* magazine.

If you're not familiar with shopper marketing, it's a relatively new marketing discipline centered on applying shopper insights to build brand demand at retail. Interest in shopper marketing has skyrocketed over the past several years, in large measure because of pressures to demonstrate the return on investment of marketing expenditures. The best and brightest marketers are increasingly recognizing that if accountability in marketing is paramount, then the mandate is to spend marketing dollars where consumers are actually opening their wallets and buying things—not while they are watching their favorite sitcom or reading their favorite magazine, but while they are shopping, at retail.

While this seems very logical, it is not as simple as it sounds. In the past, "retail" meant "in a store," but with the explosion of mobile devices, it's getting to the point where it means just about anywhere that molecules exist. This sudden and dramatic shift in shopping behavior is perhaps the greatest challenge facing marketers today, and this is precisely the issue that Liz confronted head-on in her article for the *Hub*, and has now fleshed out in the pages that follow.

The *Hub*'s mission is to explore innovation as the ultimate driver of business success, with a special focus on the retail experience as a platform for innovation. Each edition has a theme, and in the issue in which Liz's article was published, the theme was "loyalty." Some experts consider loyalty to be perhaps the most fundamental concept in business, because presumably no enterprise can survive, much less thrive, without it. The challenge of creating loyalty was the context in which Liz explored her seminal idea that advocacy is the new currency in today's socially networked world.

The conundrum, as many seasoned marketers will tell you, is that loyalty is nearly nonexistent in today's marketplace. Some, such as Dr. Byron Sharp of the Ehrenberg-Bass Institute, argue that affecting brand loyalty is effectively out of reach.

As Dr. Sharp expressed it, "Marketers don't understand loyalty. Loyalty is very important for marketers to understand in the same way it's important for engineers to understand gravity. But engineers don't talk about changing gravity. Marketers truly believe that they can change loyalty, but they can't."

Every shopper knows this to be true. Sure, we may have our preferred brands, but often—or at least every now and then—we buy whatever is cheapest. This doesn't necessarily mean that we are any less "loyal" to our preferred brands. In many categories, we have not one favorite brand that we purchase religiously, but a set of three or more acceptable products, any one of which will do. In other words, most shoppers subscribe to a rather promiscuous definition of loyalty, and there doesn't seem to be a lot that marketers can do to change this on anything like a sustainable basis.

Certainly, exceptions exist—plenty of people are totally hooked on those iPhones, that's for sure. Harley-Davidson, despite its ups and downs, still has its die-hards, and even Viva paper towels manage to attract the undying ardor of some shoppers. But brands such as these *are* exceptions. Most brands must find a way to connect with consumers from a far less rarefied place.

Ironically, for all the connectivity brought about by the digitization of media, many brands seem more disconnected than ever. The opportunities to make connections are indeed more plentiful than ever before, but it is precisely this proliferation that so often creates more noise and static, and interrupts more than it connects.

The cultural and business implications for marketers could scarcely be more profound. The fragmentation of the consumer marketplace in terms of lifestyle and media consumption isn't anything new; in fact, it's been underway for decades. The era of mass media may not be totally over, but with the rise of digital media and the increased urgency to connect with millions of shoppers on their own terms, there can be little question that the future of marketing is all about creating closer and more meaningful relationships between consumers and brands.

It's against these hard realities that I read—and the *Hub* published—Liz's white paper, which, not coincidentally, was entitled *The Shopper Economy*. In it, she addressed these many challenges and turned them on their head. Through keen insights not only into how people use these new digital media and how they shop, but, above all, into how they live their lives, Liz has rendered an important and valuable framework that forward-thinking marketers can use to connect with shoppers and build their brands in our digital world.

I won't steal Liz's thunder by saying anything more about it, except that innovation at retail is less about understanding how people shop and more about understanding how they live their lives. The future belongs to those who make the retail experience—and people's daily lives—better.

The Shopper Economy is about that future.

Tim Manners
Founder
The Hub Magazine
http://www.hubmagazine.com/

Introduction

THE VALUE OF SHOPPER BEHAVIOR

The impetus for this book came when my friends began talking about getting their kicks. They got these kicks™ by walking into a shop or scanning a bar code. But these weren't ordinary kicks. These kicks were points, redeemable at a host of retailers. My friends weren't actually *buying* anything, yet they were earning a kind of wage. This struck me as a radically different interface with commerce.

I was reminded of a book I had read a few years earlier, *The Attention Economy*. In this book, the authors explained how attention would be a unit of currency in the future. Then I saw this happening before my eyes: Facebook announced that it would pay consumers to watch advertising. But there was even more happening than had been foreseen in that book. Consumers were getting compensated for all sorts of behaviors that had become traceable digitally. With GPS, facial recognition technology, texting, and social networking, the possibilities for recording consumer behaviors had exploded—and expanded companies' opportunities to mint currencies well beyond attention.

Looking at how consumers were trading their time, attention, and behavior was a way of studying a new kind of economy: the shopper economy.

SHOPPER MARKETING EMERGES

After getting my MBA, I worked my way up through the ranks at various consumer packaged goods companies. During the years I spent learning and practicing classical brand management, the framework for shopping held fairly steady. Most of these years were in the predigital age. I remember using a calculator and a ledger sheet to forecast monthly sales data. We were still looking at shipments rather than scan data; this was a more complete way of reading the market because not all retailers had scanners (something that seems almost unimaginable today). Despite our firm's Fortune 100 status, we had only one computer for the department, and its software was so byzantine and limited that using it was hardly worth the effort. In this atmosphere, grocery shopping behavior (and the behavior of our retailer partners and competitors) remained fairly predictable. That meant that certain marketing techniques could become quite refined over time. The rate of change was slow.

Most marketers could hear the rumblings of the digital age and sensed that the storm might not be too far off. However, very few of us had any real idea what it might look like. Alvin Toffler's book *Future Shock* was cited as an indication that the rate of change, especially from a technology standpoint, would accelerate. While most of us participated in the dawning of the digital age as consumers, shoppers, and marketers, it was nonetheless a shock.

An important change was the shift to viewing the buyer as a shopper rather than a consumer. When shopping dynamics were mostly status quo, marketers could approach buyers as consumers of goods. Ad agencies dominated brand communications. Data points like consumption rates and frequency were among the brand manager's primary metrics, while redemption rates and in-store behavior were relegated to promotion houses and the trade. Sure, these metrics were important, too, but these two areas were in separate silos in most organizations. Technology in the hands of shoppers changed all that. When shoppers had access to price comparison information, peer reviews, and even inventory infor-mation, traditional marketing models began to break down. Get-ting timely messages to the shopper (not just the sit-on-the-sofa consumer) became vital for influencing her decision making and purchasing behavior. Shopper marketing, which treats buyers as shoppers along a path to purchase, emerged as an approach that was critical to marketplace success.

Shopper marketing organizations such as MARS Advertising, TracyLocke, Saatchi & Saatchi X, and a host of others linked arms with traditional ad agencies to tackle marketplace issues. The silos' walls were crumbling. This was an exciting time, and I was happy to take my brand management background into the shopper mar-keting planning function.

It was at this point in my career that I saw the new shopper currency: behavior. Just looking at the ways in which behaviors were being traded for virtual currencies, such as points, miles, or badges, fascinated me. Each behavior had a real value, and that value was the exchange rate. Shoppers evaluated the return on their efforts as either worth it or not. Shoppers themselves had become the new pay-to-play mechanism for marketing. These transactions and exchanges are the day-to-day workings of the new shopper economy.

There appear to be four primary behaviors that are used for exchange: attention, participation, advocacy, and loyalty. These four behaviors are the currencies that shoppers use to earn digital scrip, like miles or points. I call the currency of behavior *shopper currency*. I use the term *virtual currency* to mean any form of digital scrip (miles, kicks, points, eaves, bitcoins, and so on); virtual currency is redeemable for virtual and/or "real-world" goods and services.

BUILDING MARKETING STRATEGIES

This book takes the marketer's perspective and demonstrates how to leverage this new currency to meet traditional business goals. Using the framework of shopper currency, a marketer can ask: What do I want the shopper to do beyond purchase? Do I want him to:

- Pay attention?

- Engage in an activity?

- Advocate to others?

- Commit to future engagement?

Most professionals will want the shopper to do all of these things. However, realistically, most marketers need to focus their efforts by campaign, shopper target, or a short-term objective for the brand. From this perspective, we can apply marketing objectives to these questions, building strategy. For example, if I need to increase a target's awareness and consideration, I might want to give her incentives to participate in a game. Benchmarking success also becomes clearer when one kind of shopper currency is pursued in order to achieve brand goals.

Shopper currencies have financial value as well. For example, when a shopper advocates to his friends, the brand gets the value of both his stream of purchases and the stream of revenue from his converted network as well. Even at this point, it is clear that not all shopper currencies have the same value. Attention is less valuable than either loyalty or advocacy. While there are escalating values for shopper behaviors, each has utility in the marketer's toolkit. I'll talk about how and when each of them can best be used.

Shopper marketers are accustomed to building strategy using a barriers-to-purchase technique. Many obstacles can stand in the way of a purchase: lack of awareness, confusion about product usage, a perceived lack of relevance, confusion about product benefits, high price, and lack of distribution, among others. If the marketer can correctly identify and remove the barriers to purchase, the shopper will be much more likely to buy.

I apply the barriers technique to the four shopper currency behaviors. What prevents a shopper from paying attention? From participating in a program? From advocating to friends? From committing to a brand? The barriers to behavior expand on the barriers to purchase, and in some cases present very different issues. Understanding what may be preventing a shopper from advocating (for example) is key to engaging shoppers and achieving marketplace success.

In Chapter 1, I define shopper currency in greater depth, using examples and discussing emerging issues. Chapter 2 explains how the shopper is the new medium, and the implications of this. Chapters 3 and 4 review the purchase cycle and examine barriers to both purchase and behavior. The following chapters explore methods of valuing advocacy, participation, loyalty, and attention. I have included interviews with experts from companies that are leading the way forward. Also included are case studies that demonstrate how these ideas work in the real world, as well as interviews with shoppers. The final chapters offer implications for marketers and perspectives on the factors that are driving change.

The world is changing fast. Marketers are faced with a confusing explosion of tactics, vehicles, technologies, and platforms. Furthermore, the pressure to "get social" or "get mobile" is considerable. The danger here is creating activity for activity's sake. I wrote this book to create a framework for understanding how to meaningfully drive shopper behavior. The shopper economy provides a mental way in; it is a method for approaching marketing issues in the digital world, regardless of platform.

Knowing what you want shoppers to do, what stands in their way, and what these behaviors are worth are the keys to success in the shopper economy.

Foundations of the Shopper Economy

SHOPPER CURRENCY

Today there is a new currency that extends beyond the dollar. It is made possible by digital technology, and it can be minted by anyone who has a cellphone. This new currency is behavior.

In the groundbreaking book *The Attention Economy*, a Nobel Prize winner, Herbert Simon, is quoted as saying:

> What information consumes is rather obvious: it consumes the attention of its recipients. Hence a wealth of information creates a poverty of attention.

We hardly need a Nobel Prize winner to tell us that we have a poverty of attention—most of our daily lives are a testament to this. But from an economic standpoint, attention is scarce, and scarcity creates value. Attention is so valuable that it is becoming a literal medium of exchange.

Consider Virgin Mobile's Sugar Mama program. The Sugar Mama program (now ended) allowed subscribers to earn free cellphone minutes by watching and responding to ads, either online or via text message. Robert Borden, a blogger who was a user of the program, described his experience with it this way: "The first time you use the Sugar Mama site, you'll be asked to answer a few demographic questions so that they can send you targeted advertising—but this literally takes less than two minutes. After that, you'll be taken to your first ad. Most ads are in the form of videos and are about a minute long. For watching a 1 minute ad, you get 1 minute of airtime. After watching the video, you'll be asked one or two questions about what you thought of it, and then you'll be taken to a link to receive your free minute of airtime. Make sure you click this link, because if you don't you won't receive your free minute. It's as simple as that."[1] Other companies, including Facebook, Telcordia, and Alcatel-Lucent, have launched similar programs.

> *The term* shopper *has been chosen to indicate a person who is in a particular mindset or mode. A person who is in shopper mode has the intention of purchasing something, whether immediately or in the future. The shopper is engaging in a series of activities to support that transaction: becoming aware of a need, considering which products to buy, searching for outlets, deciding how to pay, and so on. Shopper marketers distinguish shoppers from consumers. Consumers are people who are engaged in consuming goods and services. It is possible that a person who is consuming information or entertainment (or just walking around) may briefly switch into shopper mode if a need is aroused or if a new brand comes into consideration.*

Let's stop here for a moment. Isn't this just old-fashioned advertising? Not really. What's different about the digital economy is that advertising morphs into a deliberate and intimate transaction. In exchange for paying attention, the shopper gets personal rewards. This isn't a frequent shopper program. It doesn't involve a purchase. Yet it directly rewards the participant—immediately and personally.

Unlike with traditional advertising, the marketer gets an additional benefit: a receipt, tangible verification that attention has been paid. The receipt in the Virgin Mobile case comes in the form of the answered questions, which the shopper texts back to a central location. By paying for a shopper's attention, the marketer has bought awareness. The marketer also got a bit of market research as part of the bargain. This is an example of a new digital transaction, paid for with behavioral currency. The behavior in this case was attention.

While *The Attention Economy* was prescient in many ways, a number of changes have taken place since the book was written more than a decade ago. Most of these changes have to do with the mass penetration and adoption of technology, notably GPS, mobile social networking, and cellphone scanning.[2] And marketers have been quick to take advantage of these developments by creating programs for shoppers. These programs involve much more than rewards for simply paying attention. Shoppers can create value with a myriad of behaviors that don't necessarily involve purchases.

Shopper currency is just this: shopper behaviors that create units of value that can be used to buy goods and services. Let's look at a few examples that extend beyond attention.

Participation

At present, Shopkick (http://www.shopkick.com/) is a front-runner in terms of sophistication in using behavioral currency. Here's how it works. A shopper downloads an app onto her cellphone. When the shopper walks into a Shopkick-participating store, her mobile device automatically records the behavior by receiving a special signal. Without further effort, the shopper has earned kicks™, which are a form of digital scrip (see Figure 1.1). (Note: The original name of the credits program was Kickbucks, but it has been shortened to kicks™.) These credits may be redeemed at hundreds of retailers and restaurants.

> *Shopper currency: Shopper behaviors that create units of value that can be used to buy goods and services.*

| Figure 1.1 | **Image of shopkick.com** |

Phil Hoops, a reporter for the *South Orange Dispatch*, described his initial experience with Shopkick, soon after its launch. "Upon entering the mall the app instantly recognized that I was inside the mall and promptly credited me with Kickbucks. Shopkick uses a special transmitter that communicates with your phone, which can determine whether or not you are actually inside a particular store. For my efforts in the mall, I earned a total of 137 Kickbucks. To put this into perspective a *Twilight* DVD costs 4400 Kickbucks and the minimum Best Buy gift certificate is valued at 500 Kickbucks. It seems that the Best Buy certificate would be within reach after a few visits to the mall. Instead of cashing in my Kickbuck points, I also was given the option of donating them towards a specific cause."[3]

Today, retailer members include Best Buy, American Eagle, Sports Authority, Crate & Barrel, Target, and many malls in New York, Los Angeles, Chicago, and San Francisco. Shopkick claims that kicks are available at more than a quarter million stores. In terms of redemption, there are many options, including iTunes, vouchers at local restaurants, gift cards at participating retailers, discounts at hundreds of small businesses, and even specific big-ticket items from major brands like Coach and Sony Bravia. These points aren't just one-off coupons good for a single purchase, but value that can accrue and be tendered at the discretion of the shopper.

Shopkick rewards behavior other than just walking into a store. Shoppers can earn points by scanning products with their cellphone. Again, purchase is not necessary. Simply scanning a designated product can earn points for the shopper.

Why would a marketer provide incentives for scanning a product without a purchase? Scanning a product means that the shopper has interacted with that brand by seeking it out and picking it up. This action proves (to the extent possible with a promotion) that the shopper has given consideration to the marketer's brand.

For bigger-ticket items, where product sampling and trial aren't feasible, this is a good marketing technique.

So far, we have seen two behaviors being rewarded directly: paying attention and participating (here, walking into stores or scanning products). It seems that from a shopper marketing perspective, walking into a store is more valuable than paying attention. Why? Because a shopper is more likely to buy a product while he is in a store (even if that store is digital, but more on that later). Further, scanning a product puts that brand into the shopper's hand, while paying attention does not. So, again it seems that scanning is more valuable than paying attention. It appears that shopper currency has escalating value, from a marketer's perspective.

> *Shopper currency has escalating denominations.*

Advocacy

A third valuable behavior is advocating. This behavior may be more valuable to the marketer than either paying attention or participating, because it opens a network of *new* shoppers. This behavior extends beyond the single shopper or the one-off purchase. Think of this category as a continuum, from simple sharing to brand evangelism.

Consumers are given options to quickly and easily share commercial messaging with their networks all the time—posting an item on Digg, tweeting a link, posting on Facebook, blogging, hitting a "like" button, and a host of other mechanisms. There are incentives for some of this sharing. For example, Rimmel cosmetics offered a discount coupon on a new product if the shopper hit the "like" button. But many, even most, sharing opportunities do not have incentives at this time. Consumers share in order to gain social prestige ("I'm in the know") or to offer something that they believe would be relevant to a select group of friends.

Tasti D-Lite created a very savvy program to provide incentives for sharing with social networks. Max Chafkin in *INC.* magazine described the program: "In January [2010], the company began asking its customers to turn over their Twitter account information as part of Tasti D-Lite's loyalty program. . . . Fifty points gets a customer a free medium cone or cup. To get points for tweeting, a customer submits his Twitter username and password. Then, every time he buys something at a store, he swipes a loyalty card at the register. Tasti D-Lite's point-of-sale system automatically logs in to his Twitter account and sends a tweet informing his followers of the purchase. 'I just earned 9 TastiRewards points at Tasti D-Lite New Rochelle.'"[4]

> Tasti D-Lite: When a customer swipes a loyalty card at the POS, the system logs onto the shopper's Twitter account and tweets his followers: "I just earned 9 TastiReward points at Tasti D-Lite."

Sharing "likes" with social networks is advocacy "lite." Real advocating takes sharing one step further; it is endorsing the brand personally and aligning one's reputation with the brand. Hitting the "+1" button, tweeting a link, or sharing on Digg is valuable. But personally urging a friend to buy or taking the time to write a positive review has a bigger financial impact on the brand. In fact, WSL Strategic Retail (http://www.wslstrategicretail.com/) reports that reviews influence actual purchasing more than tweets or "likes" at a ratio of 2:1.[5]

Location-based social networks are most important for retailer advocacy at this point. The reason is that people are seeking friendship and connection, and the retailers benefit as the hosts of the party. Here's how it works:

Download the foursquare app (https://foursquare.com/) onto your smartphone. Find your friends. You can use Facebook, Gmail, or Twitter to find your friends who are already on foursquare (the program automatically finds them for you). Now you are ready to begin checking into locations. Check-ins can happen anywhere—from the gym to coffee shops to schools and even on the road. When you check into a place more often than anyone else, you become the "mayor" of that location.

By becoming mayor, you earn a badge. There are many other kinds of badges you can earn, too: the swarm badge, the adventurer badge, the explorer badge, the I'm-on-a-boat! badge, and hundreds of others. The badges (and a few other digital tokens) are units of value.

Entertainment properties have hopped on this bandwagon. There are Bravo-, MTV-, and CNN-themed badges. Bravo TV celebrities, such as those from *Top Chef Masters*, recommend various local places for foursquare users to check in, including restaurants, stores, and events. Imagine hosting a series of branded events across the country, like wine tastings at Morton's or local produce fairs at farmers' markets. Not only can you provide direct incentives for participation, but your customers can invite their friends to meet them there—with turn-by-turn directions. These are opportunities for advocacy like never before.

I did a blog scrape to get a better understanding of why people use it regularly. I found this explanation from a veteran: "I'd consider myself a heavy user of geolocation services (621 check-ins over 233 nights out). I use foursquare to add a layer of information to the world around me. Often as I'm finishing dinner out or a meeting downtown, I'll check to see who's around. Checking in (and having friends that check in) has led to many shared drinks, meals and cabs. I've also discovered events that were happening (attended by friends) in my town or in other places I've visited when I had a free evening."

Foursquare, or any mobile social network, can be used to implement a marketing program involving shopper currency. Foursquare is an example of advocating because of the way it is used by its denizens. It adds a layer of personal information, namely, the location of the user's friends and places of interest. If I invite my friends to meet me at a mall or a restaurant, that is an endorsement of that venue or an alignment of my brand with it. If I am the mayor of a downtown Starbucks, that is a hearty endorsement of that brand. I am actively advocating that brand, broadcasting that fact to my social network, and (implicitly and sometimes explicitly) inviting the members of that network to join me there. This is not the only mechanism for advocacy, but it is one that showcases some of the digital technology coming our way.

Loyalty

Both the Tasti D-Lite and the foursquare examples show that the marketer has commissioned advocacy, as well as trip frequency. This brings us to another question: What about loyalty? Traditional, passive *cents-off* programs aren't the same as earning scrip for simply behaving. Discounting price without requiring behavior is a sale. However, true loyalty behavior does have a place in behavioral currency because it involves shopper commitment. Frequent flyer miles, American Express points, and Kroger card points are examples of scrip used to incent commitment.

It may seem that the digital economy is overstated here a bit. The platforms supporting these programs are not uniformly available or used. But the point is that the ubiquity of digital communications is radically changing our lives, including marketing interactions. As William Gibson famously said, "The future is already here—it's just not very evenly distributed."

ESCALATING VALUE

We have described four types of shopper currency. Each type of behavior represents increasing value to the marketer. However, the continuum of worth from attention to advocacy is rough. There will be cases in which participation will yield better financial results than advocating. For example, certain personal-care products may be too embarrassing for an advocacy program. In such cases, marketers would want to engage shoppers directly through a participation program. In other cases, advocating may be more valuable than loyalty, for example, in categories with very long purchase cycles, such as appliances. The relative worth of these behaviors needs to be measured on a brand-by-brand basis, according to the marketing objectives. Thinking of these behaviors as having different units of worth is useful to a businessperson who needs to provide incentives to shoppers, as well as tally the cost of a whole program against an estimated profit.

Shopper currency has escalating value: attention, participation, advocacy, and loyalty.

Furthermore, the absolute value of advocacy, or any behavior, will also vary from category to category. Several market research studies are already beginning to demonstrate this. An excellent report by WSL Strategic Retail[6] measured the impact of social networks on buying behavior. It created an SI score, or a social influence score, based on hundreds of surveys. The study shows that the impact of advocacy and social networks indeed varies by category. The SI score for computers and software is a hefty 68, while the

SI score for health products such as prescriptions and OTC drugs scored a 44. So, OTC marketers may not be as interested in investing in advocacy programs as marketers of electronics.

Real Currency

Why is this currency? Aren't these just ways to execute promotions? These examples are promotions. However, digital technology adds another dimension to the transaction, converting shopper behavior into fungible currency. Digital technology enables virtual currencies because it can record behaviors, translate them into earnings, and store and bank the value, which can then be redeemed across channels and platforms.

In terms of recording, all of these behaviors can be verified and documented. A special transmitter enables Shopkick to verify whether a shopper is in fact standing in a particular store. At some point, GPS may be able to do the same thing. Simple texting lets advertisers verify that a viewer has seen an ad. Alternatively, facial recognition technology could do the same thing. Scanning allows marketers to verify that their shoppers have indeed picked up the product, and sending messages to social networks is easily confirmed as well. Identifying a user and her tracking behavior on a mobile device or laptop (or soon with ambient computing) is a no-brainer. Technology allows various receipts so that marketers know that the debt has been paid. The implication is that not only is ROI easier to determine than with traditional TV or print, but also offers and messages can be measured and optimized in real time, as well as be very specifically targeted.

The accurate accrual and recording of value makes "earning" really possible. Shopper currency, or shopper labor, is most often repaid with virtual currency, which for our purposes is any form of digital scrip.[7] In this book, virtual currency includes everything from Facebook Credits to WoW Gold to store gift cards to coupons to Bitcoins to frequent buyer points to Eaves.

Value can be stored in such a way that it is visible to the seller, the banker, and the shopper. A shopper who has access to stored value can spend those resources when he sees fit. Importantly, stored value needs to be recognized by merchants in order to be redeemed and therefore retain its worth. One of the reasons Shopkick is successful is that many merchants are recognizing kicks™ points. At the end of the day, the virtual currency winner will be the one that is recognized by the broadest group of companies.

Today, American Express Membership Rewards points is probably the front-runner. However, it is intriguing to think about the newly minted Facebook Credits as a potential force in the future. The sheer size of the Facebook user base (see Figure 1.2) would give some weight and cachet to the currency. However, these credits would need to be recognized beyond the virtual realm to become a viable supplement to fiat currency.

Figure 1.2	**Facebook's Population**

facebook's population
ranked 3rd in the world.

	1. China	1,336,450,000		1. Brazil	192,651,000
	2. India	1,178,436,000		2. Pakistan	169,010,500
	3. Facebook	400,000,000		3. Bangladesh	162,221,000
	4. United States	308,898,000		4. Nigeria	154,729,000
	5. Indonesia	231,369,500		5. Russia	141,927,297

Data Source: Wikipedia   Design: TechXav/Zhou Tong
2011
Source: Wikipedia. "Because Wikipedia content is distributed under an open license, anyone can reuse, or re-distribute it at no charge."

The point is this: insofar as digital scrip is recognized across channels and platforms, it is "real" currency for shoppers' purposes. This brings us to the overall nature of the shopper economy.

The New Marketplace

Let's put shopper currency in a larger economic context. Because technology is allowing us to expand our units of exchange, the marketplace for transactions has expanded, too. Buyers and sellers have more options in terms of *what* they can spend to acquire goods, services, and other assets.

In the schematic in Figure 1.3, each box lists the forms of currency that are available to the entity at the top of the box—either buyer or seller. The internal arrows indicate the exchanges that are most frequent today. Starting at the top, the first arrow shows consumers spending billions of dollars in hard cash to buy traditional merchandise, like groceries. The second arrow shows that virtual currency is also used to buy traditional goods and services, like redeeming a coupon or frequent flyer points. Virtual currency is also used to buy virtual goods, such as enhancements for World of Warcraft, FooPets, or FarmVille.

The third arrow shows that shoppers will labor for virtual currency, like earning Facebook Credits for watching an ad. Consumers will also work to earn soft currencies like branded entertainment or convenience. For example, consumers participate by surrendering some personal information in exchange for convenience. Personal information is a big bartering chip that shoppers hold in their hands. For purposes of this book, disclosing personal information is captured by participation.

It is interesting to note that buyer currencies are roughly the same as seller currencies, in terms of the possibilities for exchange. However, each entity prioritizes its assets differently, and each has different motivations as well. A shopper may seek to be entertained (the soft currency of sponsored content) while standing in line, whereas a commercial entity doesn't need to assuage its boredom. Buyers want to enhance their feelings and their pocketbooks, whereas brands are primarily seeking financial rewards.

The exchange rates of virtual currencies against hard currencies is a hot topic. There have been reports of Chinese prisoners being forced to play World of Warcraft and other games to "mine gold." The inmates work all day on construction projects and then work at night playing games. Allegedly, the guards redeem the virtual currency for hard currency, and so make a profit on the backs of the prisoners. The sheer fact that this *could be* happening points to the value of virtual versus hard currencies. The prisoners earn more by playing games than they do in construction projects, and so the guards have financial incentives.

| Figure 1.3 | **Buyer and Seller Currencies** |

Buyer Currencies

- Hard Currency ($, €, etc.)
- Virtual Currency (Miles, Coupons, Scrip)
- Shopper Currencies (Labor, Behavior)
  - Attention
  - Participation
  - Sharing—Advocacy
  - Loyalty
- Goods/Services (Barter)

Seller Currencies

- Goods/Services (Virtual/Traditional)
- Virtual Currency (Miles, Coupons, Scrip)
- Soft Currency (Sponsored Content, Apps, Intangibles)
  - Social Status
  - Access
  - Information
  - Entertainment
  - Convenience
  - Altruism
- Hard Currency (Cash Back, Rebates)

Wages for Eyeballs

Facebook offers users a chance to get paid to watch ads. When a user watches an ad, he earns credit, which is automatically deposited into his Facebook account. The credits may be redeemed within online games. Here's how it works:

> Users click on an icon "Earn Free Credits" or something similar. This will open a video player which users click to start. At the end of the video, Credits are deposited into the user's account, and they are given the choice of following links to websites or Facebook Pages for the advertiser, or filling out an optional poll. They can then spend their Credits in that game or any other that supports Credits as a payment system—which will be all games on the Facebook Platform starting July 1st when Credits become mandatory. ("Facebook Deepens Partnership with TrialPay DealSpot to Offer Credits for Watching Videos," Inside Facebook, May 5, 2011.)

Gamers love their games. They gleefully while away hours, days, and weeks playing and obsessing about playing. These aren't just teenage boys, either. Many a middle-aged suburban matron is riveted by her FarmVille creation. Offering credits for in-game goods seems like a real boon for gamers of all stripes. In addition, credits may be redeemed for other value elsewhere. More revenue for game developers, more eyeballs for advertisers, and more goods for users. What's not to love?

According to an insightful article in Fast Company, there is a downside. What is done gleefully for free is done begrudgingly for wages. "The last thing they [Facebook executives] want is users dreading the number of times they have to log in and watch ads to buy that new-fangled virtual product they've *been eyeing. It replaces enjoyment with boredom, anxiety, and resentment," says Gregory Ferenstein, digital reporter. ("Facebook Paying Users for Ad Views: The Good, the Bad, and the Psychologically Ugly,"* Fast Company, *May 9, 2011.)*

While this is certainly a concern, including the ensuing schemes that users will find to earn credits while not watching ads, there is a bigger issue for the industry. If marketers make it a habit to pay users to watch ads, participate, or advocate, there may be no going back. Consumers might begin to assume that payment is part of their earned rights as an audience.

The implication is that paying consumers will become an expense of any digital marketing campaign (advertisement, promotion, or other). Because of pressure on ROI performance and shrinking budgets overall, this expense puts another nail in the coffin of "traditional" media—that is, until "traditional" media morph into their next incarnation, which will probably include virtual currency mechanisms and social networking dimensions.

As virtual currencies begin to command consistent exchange rates against geopolitical currencies, we will be able to see a new way of valuing everything, including labor.

In fact, the whole labor and budget of marketing is shifting away from third parties and toward the shopper herself. The shopper is doing the marketing labor herself by agreeing to watch ads, participate in programs, share with others, and sell the product. These are auto-advertisements and auto-promotions. The implication is that, increasingly, marketing budgets will shift toward paying the shopper directly.

In some sense, shoppers are earning wages from the seller by agreeing to share in the labor of marketing. If this is so, why aren't we talking about a simple dollar wage? That is an interesting question and the subject of the next chapter.

CHAPTER 1 Recap: *Foundations of the Shopper Economy*

- Shopper currency is shopper behaviors that create units of value that can be redeemed for goods and services.
- There are four denominations of shopper currency:
  - Attention
  - Participation
  - Advocacy
  - Loyalty
- The digital era has expanded the currencies available to both the buyer and the seller.
  - For the seller, these include goods and services (virtual and conventional), virtual currency (miles, points, coupons, and scrip), soft currency (sponsored content and intangibles), and hard currency (cash rebates).
  - For the buyer, these include hard currency ($,€), virtual currency (miles, coupons, and scrip), shopper currencies (labor and behavior), and goods/professional services (barter).

2

The Shopper Is the Medium

Historically, brands have paid huge sums of money to place advertising on television, in magazines, on the radio, and in stores. Today, advertising monies also go toward banner ads, viral video ads, pop-up ads, and various mobile messages, among others.

Increasingly, at least some of the marketing budget needs to be allocated to the shoppers themselves. This isn't just for traditional promotional expenses like coupon redemption. This new expense in the marketer's budget goes directly to the shoppers in exchange for their marketing labor. Shopper behavior, beyond simple purchase, is pivotal to the success of any twenty-first-century marketing campaign. And the reason is simple: the shopper is the new medium.

Let's think about a person as a medium to reach others. Some people will have a more extensive social network than others. These people have been called a variety of names: super connectors (*Never Eat Alone, and Other Secrets to Success, One Relationship at a Time*, Keith Ferrazzi and Tahl Raz, Crown Business 2005), WOMBATs ("Word-of-Mouth Believers and Transmitters," Iconoculture http://www.iconoculture.com/), and influentials (*The Influentials: One American in Ten Tells the Other Nine How to Vote, Where to Eat, and What to Buy,* Jon Berry and Ed Keller, Free Press, 2003), among others. While there are some differences in the definitions of these superconnected, influential, self-appointed advocates, many marketers agree that advocates are important. Social rating systems like Klout have sprung up so that advertisers can easily identify and recruit their best super connectors.

In fact, the socially "contagious" nature of depression, obesity, and happiness has been documented. However, there are some social theorists who suggest that the super connector–type model is not an accurate depiction of how social contagion spreads. The discussion on this issue is extensive. However, as a practical matter, shoppers will be increasingly important in spreading brand messages, whether through key influentials or through other seeding mechanisms.

As marketers recruit shoppers to work for them, the budget and labor of marketing will shift directly to the shopper. The shopper is the marketer's new "pay-to-play" mechanism.

EACH SHOPPER IS A BRAND

People are brands in their own right. They feel that they have an image to uphold, or one that they want to try to create. Look at the hours people spend creating avatars, uploading pictures of themselves on Facebook, and tweeting their smallest movement ("I'm having my morning coffee!"). The *New York Times* reported a new phenomenon, FOMO, or "fear of missing out." It "refers to the blend of anxiety, inadequacy and irritation that can flare up while skimming social media like Facebook, Twitter, foursquare, and Instagram. Billions of Twitter messages, status updates and photographs provide *thrilling glimpses of the daily lives* and activities of friends, 'frenemies,' coworkers and peers."[1]

Since time immemorial, people have been concerned with their self-image and looking good to their peers. However, until recently, most people didn't have the means to actually broadcast themselves. This brings more pressure to bear on presenting one's best image. There is a phrase in the vernacular now, "Facebook ready," which means looking one's best. And if one doesn't look one's best (say, a friend posted an indiscreet picture), there are mechanisms to clean things up, such as the "Wisk-It" application on Facebook. This app helps users scrub photos. If this isn't enough, some people opt for the more serious Reputation-

Brands must persuade shoppers to advocate for them. Using shoppers as media without their permission understandably outrages them.

In 2007, Facebook launched Beacon, an opt-out program that broadcast information about users' activities and purchases on the web without their permission. Facebook users were up in arms and filed a lawsuit. Facebook was forced to back down. It pulled the program in 2009.

Again in 2011, Facebook apologized after globally launching a facial-recognition technology without asking its users to opt in. The technology aided "tagging," or linking photos with names. Users were given the choice of opting out, but not everyone was aware of this. Graham Cluley, a senior consultant with the security firm Sophos, said that users' annoyance was less about the product's purpose than about the manner in which it was made live.

"Once again Facebook seems to be sharing personal information by default," said Mr. Cluley.[2]

Defender, a paid service that cleans up images, text, and references for its clients.

Since people care this much about maintaining their digital persona, they also care about which brands they are seen using and which ones they advocate. Therefore, the shopper as a medium is different from, say, television as a medium. With the exception of some adult-only brands, in general, it's relatively easy for a brand to keep its message intact in a televised context. In that context, brands don't have to consider too much, beyond public decency and paying the bill.

On the other hand, the shopper medium is different. Brands need to pass muster with their advocates. In order to be *worthy* of advocacy, brands need to have some prestige (Mercedes-Benz), social cachet (Seventh Generation paper products), or halo association of cool (Apple). In other words, the brand needs to offer some modest value to the advocate personally in order to earn an endorsement. That's because a shopper is a brand in her own right. She needs to know that the brand she is promoting to her friends (and even people she hasn't met) won't make her look like a fool. Furthermore, it must enhance her image in some small way. Your brand must align with her brand.

THE EVOLUTION OF TOOLS

The seller's traditional tools have included advertising (such as television, print, radio, and outdoor), promotions (couponing, sweepstakes, games, and so on), and in-store communications (including signage, sampling, and displays).

Television, as a "lean back" medium, has been faulted at times for being a bit of a blunt instrument for marketers. Viewers who are leaning back on the sofa are pretty passive. They may or may not be watching at all, even if TV ads are playing in the same room. TV ads aren't very discriminating; they broadcast to anyone who is in the room, and that room can be a waiting room or some type of public area. TV ads can be skipped, using TiVo and other mechanisms. The big appeal of television, of course, has been its reach. But while Americans watch plenty of TV, the number of channels and the amount of content they can choose from is multiplying continually. Audiences are more fragmented than ever. While fragmentation helps narrow the target, television today is still primarily a business-to-consumer mass effort.[3]

Reaching viewers on other screens—laptops, notebooks, or mobiles—is a business-to-consumer personalized effort. Digital advertising is exciting because of the extreme personalization of the medium. Marketers can talk to each customer as an individual in real time.

In 1993, the consulting team of Peppers and Rogers wrote a prescient book called *The One-to-One Future*. In it, they described a brave new world of marketing that was different from the mass marketing of television and print. "Technology has brought us back to a way of doing business by making it possible to remember relationships with individual customers—sometimes millions of them—one at a time."[4]

Beyond business-to-consumer mass and business-to-consumer personalized, peer-to-peer messaging is often the most compelling in terms of conversion. The marketer may reach a smaller audience, but the audience is usually more easily converted because the message is coming from a trusted source. In peer-to-peer commercial communications, the role of the brand is to be the gas in the engine, rather than the engine itself. News, entertainment, and incentives can help fuel peer-to-peer commercial messaging. However, consumers also create their own communications about brands without incentives or pass along content from the brand.

Table 2.1 shows some examples of how commercial communications have evolved. This is not meant to be an exhaustive list of every possible type of message, or to espouse any particular theory, but simply to demonstrate key changes over time.

Table 2.1	Evolution of Communication Tools		
	B-to-C, Mass	**B-to-C, Personalized**	**C-to-C, Peer to Peer**
Role of Shopper	Shopper is receiving brand information, along with everyone else	Shoppers have opted-into the brand and have surrendered some information	Shoppers get advertising and promotions through their friends
Advertising	TV Spot Print Ad Radio Spot	Personalized Banner and Pop-up Ads; Opted-in Mobile Ads, Interactive TV Ads with Opt-in Features	Meebo, foursquare, Gifting, Facebook posting, Tweeting, Likes, E-mail "sharing," Peer reviews in Angie's List, Yelp, DIGG, StumbleUpon
Out-of-Home Ads	Billboard: "Eat At Joe's"	Personalized location-based, mobile ad: "Turn Left to Eat at Joe's"	Yelp Mobile Review: "Order the Roast Beef at Joe's"
Promotions	FSI's in Newspapers; Store Circulars	Coupons delivered to your inbox from the Brand; specific coupons on your shopper card by your buying patterns (direct mail or e-mail) Shopkick Interactive	Peer-to-Peer Groupon discounts; In-Game peer-to-peer promotions
Store Events	Store-Wide Sale	Text Alert on Mobile: "SEARS Shoe Sale Now!" Inbox Personalized Sale: "We have replacement dishes for your pattern available."	Foursquare; Flash Mobs; Mobile Groupon Invitations from friends

While Table 2.1 very broadly depicts an evolution of commercial communication, mass messaging won't disappear. Pencils and pens weren't replaced by the computer or mobile devices. Pens are still useful in other ways. Remember the predictions of a "paperless" society? The point is that many older technologies live comfortably alongside newer technologies. For example, while many digital signs are already interactive, a traditional billboard will continue to be useful to marketers because of its unique and specific advantages.

The most interesting part of this evolution is the explosion of possibilities created by the most recent two categories. With these two types of communication, marketers can shift the labor to shoppers directly, on an individual basis, creating *self-serve* promotions and advertising on a fairly large scale.

EACH SHOPPER IS A MEDIA VEHICLE

As we have noted, the shopper is a brand, but he is also a media vehicle. First, he is a media vehicle for himself. For example, when he participates in Shopkick, he is engaging in a kind of do-it-yourself promotion or self-serve promotion. In some sense, this is a cultural extension of the self-checkout. Shoppers are assuming the labor of the cash-wrap function in grocery stores. In airports, passengers are assuming the labor of checking in, either at the kiosk or on their mobiles. In the financial world, ATMs are self-service banking (and many of their functions are also available as mobile self-service banking). So, Shopkick and its competitor Check-Points are the self-service version of brand promotions: pick up and scan the product yourself. The sales assistant can be disintermediated with some kinds of auto-promotions.

> Shopkick alert: "Today only, collect 200 kicks for walking into your nearest @BestBuy store. Valid at all Best Buy stores nationwide!" Twitter @ Shopkick, May 25, 2011.

Second, he is a media vehicle for his network and for other shoppers. There has always been word of mouth, but today, shoppers can broadcast pictures, audio, and text to thousands, and even millions, of others around the world in real time. A brand advocate is literally worth more today than he was in the past because he has real reach. This is do-it-yourself advocacy. The future of advertising, at least in part, is in the hands of these new media vehicles. And they will expect to be compensated for their efforts.

SELF-SERVE PROMOTIONS

Self-serve promotions shift the labor and budget of marketing directly onto the shopper. In the promotions we will be discussing in this section, a shopper decides to pay attention and/or participate (shopper currency) in a branded program in exchange for some sort of compensation from the seller. This is shopper labor for wages.

Usually the shopper is earning virtual currency, such as points, miles, credits, or some other form of digital scrip. The seller also uses softer currencies like entertainment or information to make participation emotionally rewarding. This buyer-seller transaction can be tracked in Figure 1.3.

Let's look at a few examples of self-serve promotions. We've been talking a lot about Shopkick because it is one of the first widespread shopper platforms available. Every day, Shopkick tweets opportunities to participate to its user base. In the spring of 2011, it invited shopkickers to earn 200 kicks for walking into a Best Buy store. The promotion was designed to get shoppers to consider products from Best Buy, probably to help the chain capture Father's Day and graduation gift purchases. The compensation for taking that action was in Shopkick's branded virtual currency. Most brands that offer virtual currencies in exchange for self-serve promotions must carry the actual expense of the scrip on their books. This is a genuine financial transaction.

Once in the store, the shopper can scan products to earn more points. This kind of promotion is driving *brand consideration* as never before. Shoppers are being rewarded for finding the product in the aisle, picking it up, and turning it over. This is a great example of a self-serve promotion—no sales associate is selling here. The interaction is between the shopper and the brand, with Shopkick serving as a platform. Also, this case demonstrates that self-serve promotions can extend beyond buy-to-get loyalty programs.

A softer currency like fun and entertainment is usually part of the equation as well. Shopkick has an animated character named Buck, which is a device to drive more participation. Sticking with Father's Day self-serve promotions as an example, Buck extended play as an element: "Today is our Father's Day Hunt! Help Buck find the 3 gifts hidden in 3 shops to earn an exclusive badge (the Father's Day badge) that you'll get tomorrow evening!"[5]

Shoppers—yes, adults—spent time surfing around the site trying to find the three gifts in order to earn the badge. We can believe that people spent time doing this because of the lengthy trail of commentary by shoppers.

Using entertainment as an incentive to participate works well among many segments. From FarmVille addicts to Angry Birds players, consumers use games to fight boredom. According to the Pew Internet & American Life Project, "Some 69% of teen cell owners agreed with the statement: 'When I am bored, I use my cell phone to entertain myself.' This is especially true of girls. Some 77% of them say cell phones are good boredom killers, compared with 61% of boys."[6] The same report noted that nearly 40 percent of adults also use their mobiles to combat boredom.

Quick digital handheld games have their place: while waiting in line for a plane, sitting in a restaurant, watching TV, or just bored while doing something else. Marketers are learning that "gamification" of commercial apps attracts participation. "'Gamification' is the process of using game thinking and game mechanics to engage users and solve problems," says Gabe Zichermann, coauthor of the book *Game-Based Marketing* and chairman of the Gamification Summit (http://gamification.co/gabe-zichermann/).[7]

Zichermann cites *The Biggest Loser* as an example of the gamification of weight loss. It's much more fun to earn rewards and recognition than to diet and punitively deprive oneself of food. Look at Louisville, Kentucky. It ranks in the top 10 most-obese cities in the United States, with more than six in ten adults qualifying as seriously overweight. Throughout 2008, there was a public campaign touting the benefits of physical exercise, yet according to the *New York Times*, during the period when this campaign was going on, obesity rates and inactivity continued to rise.[8] Louisville has done a good job of revitalizing some of its bike paths and sidewalks in an effort to encourage physical activity. While this kind of infrastructure is very good, it may be only laying the foundation for behavioral change, without really prompting it. What if public funds were used to create a digital game in which participants could sign up to compete? Participants could track and post their weight, exercise, and calorie consumption, along with progress pictures. As a reward, winners could get their pictures on billboards around the city and also get a tax rebate. My hunch is that this approach would generate better compliance with the stated goals of the program.

Of course gamification brings us to kids. Kids are a ready-made audience for gamified content. They love to play games and have throughout recorded history. Today's kids are digital natives—those intuitive digital denizens who coach mom and dad on how to program their televisions, download apps, and use mobile social networks.

Importantly, millennials have grown up "snacking" on media, and this has primed them for gamified commercial content. *WIRED* magazine described media snacking this way: "We now devour our pop culture the same way we enjoy candy and chips—in conveniently packaged bite-size nuggets made to be munched easily with increased frequency and maximum speed. This is snack culture—and boy, is it tasty (not to mention addictive)."[9]

Self-serve promotions can be gamified media snacks. It's no surprise that kids are getting an onslaught of enticements to play and interact with brands in this way.

Cereal brands have great game content for kids. Kids are captive audiences in many circumstances, but breakfast time is a classic. It's the perfect time to play. On the back of a box of Honey Nut Cheerios cereal, there is a game involving a character named the Honey Defender. This game can be played without a computer or a mobile. However, one morning I sat with my seven-year-old niece over breakfast, and I saw her get up and carry the box to the computer. She typed in the URL on the back of the box. There was Honey Defender! She played the game on the spot. In the upper left-hand corner is a blue flag that announces, "Hey kids, this is Advertising!"[10]

I wonder how Honey Defender is different from, say, playing with digital dolls on barbie.com. Barbie doesn't announce that any of its games are advertising because it is a destination site for play. However, as a practical matter, I am not sure that the two are much different to my niece.

American Girl is one of the best integrations of online play and nondigital merchandising. The brand has a featured girl of the year online, complete with a story, activities, games, wallpaper, and more. Of course, after playing online, all of the nondigital merchandise, from books to dolls to wardrobe, is available for purchase. In this sense, it falls into the self-serve promotion bucket. It is a branded activity that engages shoppers to consider purchasing. Of course, it is also plain fun to play.

I am not against providing branded content to children in a digital context, even if that content is subtly geared to sell product. Here's why: this has been happening for decades in the predigital world. The "nag" factor has always been a lever for marketers. Even the iconic Cracker Jack had a prize that a child could play with after the snack was eaten. The prize may have reminded more than one child to ask for Cracker Jack again. Decoder rings in cereal boxes also provided a primitive gamified branded interaction with children—and probably to the same effect: "Mom, I need the other piece to complete the treasure hunt!"

SELF-SERVE *LOYALTY* PROGRAMS

So far we've seen how self-serve promotions can solicit attention and participation from shoppers. Let's look at a few programs where shoppers trade loyalty (shopper currency) for some sort of compensation from the seller.

Real loyalty is weightier than simply taking advantage of a buy-more-get-more promotion. It is a commitment to buy more in the future because the buyer is aligned with the benefits of the brand. In this sense, it is a behavioral or shopper currency. Buyers who are loyal to functional benefits are casual friends of the brand. On the other hand, passionate buyers seek the emotional, social, or even spiritual benefits of the brand. For example, there are people who have the Harley-Davidson logo tattooed on their arms. That's passion. There are people who buy lululemon athletica because they are aligned with the philosophy of the brand. This philosophy is embodied in the lululemon manifesto, which is printed on the side of every shopping bag. It espouses affirmations such as, "Success is determined by how you handle setbacks" and, "Do one thing a day that scares you." People who are spiritually aligned with a brand don't need scrip. They need deep reasons to continue to align their identities with the brand philosophy.

Often passionate brand loyalists can be converted into advocates. However, we'll see later that the bulk of the financial return from advocates comes from moderate users of the brand, rather than the heaviest users. So it makes sense to separate loyalty programs from advocacy programs.

Loyalty programs that reward buyers with virtual currency are probably the most prevalent form of self-serve promotion. Examples are everywhere, and many have become very sophisticated at this point. Granddaddy examples include frequent flyer miles and American Express points. Most banks today also have virtual currency reward programs, where a debit card user can accrue value for purchasing with the card. Most often this is scrip, but it sometimes can be hard currency in the form of cents-back savings programs or college funds. There are also opportunities to gift scrip to friends, family, or charity as well.

Frequent shopper cards are widely accepted loyalty mechanisms, including those at CVS, Stop & Shop, Kroger, Safeway, and a host of others. Today, most shoppers have a few scannable plastic tags on their key rings. Every time a shopper goes to the register in a brick-and-mortar store, her card is swiped and the discounts are applied. While the card creates a direct relationship with each shopper, most card programs aren't reaching their potential as real loyalty drivers.

Jeff Weidauer, vice president of marketing at Vestcom (http://www.vestcom.com/) and one of the original designers of shopper loyalty cards, explains a few of the core issues. "The problem is that shoppers use the cards to be sure that they are getting the discounted price shown at the shelf or on the circular. However, they aren't aware of any benefits beyond price. Shoppers haven't seen higher-level benefits with their shopper cards." In some cases, using a shopper card will also generate points for the buyer. However, how these points may be redeemed isn't always clear to the shopper.

There is a further issue here. Shopper cards reward buyers with retailer-only points; debit or credit cards reward buyers with another system of points. It is possible that a dominant virtual currency may emerge or that clearinghouse sites will offer exchange rates for all manner of currencies.

DO-IT-YOURSELF ADVOCACY PROGRAMS AND PASS-ALONG PROMOTIONS

There are a plethora of mechanisms that allow shoppers to share, review, and recommend brands. As often as not, shoppers don't seek virtual currency or any compensation from the brand. This is because they are aligned with the brand, and the softer social currency of "being in the know" is sufficient compensation.

Here's a partial list of sharing and advocacy devices today:

- A "like" or "+1" button

- Become a "Fan"

- Post to Facebook (or some other) Wall

- Pass along a viral video (YouTube)

- Tweet and retweet

- Tweet *within* LinkedIn or some other network

- Share mobile content with a personal network (like a product pic) using LIBOX

- Generate product reviews and star ratings (mostly retailer and brand sites)

- Review and rate on Yelp

- Share commentary on foursquare, Loopt, or Meebo

- Share via Digg, StumbleUpon, or other such sites

- "Gift"

- Pass-along discounts and coupons (send-a-friend programs)

- Post an Affiliate Widget (Groupon, Amazon, and others)

- E-mail one's contacts

The list of possible mechanisms for sharing, reviewing, and recommending expands and morphs weekly. The choices reflect a spectrum of emotional intensity from blasé (a "like" button) to passionate (a Yelp review and rating).

While it may be most desirable to convert consumers into unpaid passionate advocates, this may not always be possible. Rewarding a recommender doesn't have to be a bribe, either. It can be a simple thank you, like a party favor. Groupon, for example, rewards advocacy. If I invite new friends onto Groupon, I get $10 in Groupon Bucks. The payback on this investment is probably quite handsome because of the future sales to the recruited shoppers. According to *McKinsey Quarterly*, "Marketing induced consumer-to-consumer word of mouth generates more than twice the sales of paid advertising in categories as diverse as skincare and mobile phones."[11]

Compensation for advocacy can also scale up to a business-partner level with real profit sharing too, like the Groupon Affiliates program. This is a program designed for bloggers and entrepreneurs with websites. Those who post a Groupon widget on their site get a percentage of revenue every time a visitor buys something.

Of course, children are laboring as brand advocates as well. In the United Kingdom and elsewhere, there are activists who are campaigning against this phenomenon. "Under most schemes, children are given extra 'points' if they talk positively about the brands on Twitter, Facebook or other social networking sites. These points can be traded in for merchandise or tickets to pop concerts."[12]

I don't believe this is inherently evil. For example, Handip-oints.com is a website that allows kids to earn virtual currency for real-world chores that their parents assign. The kids can redeem the points for virtual goods in digital games, or, with parents' permission, they can be accumulated toward a real-world DVD of Hannah Montana or a Star Wars Wii game.

There is a site called Couponing to Disney that shows moms how to use coupons on participating brands in order to save for a trip to Disney World. On June 15, 2011, one featured coupon was from the Chili's restaurant chain, "Chili's Kids Eat FREE Today!"[13]

These last two examples show parental involvement. So, perhaps the real issue isn't whether kids are spending their shopper currency participating or promoting, but the role brands play.

CHAPTER 2 Recap: *The Shopper Is the Medium*

- The shopper is the new medium for marketers.
  - Word of mouth isn't what it used to be. Shoppers reach thousands, even millions of others through a host of digital mechanisms, making each person a media vehicle in his own right.
  - Giving shoppers effective incentives to advocate will be critical to a brand's success. Shoppers look for soft rewards like the social status that comes from "being in the know" or for virtual currencies, like points.
  - This exchange makes shoppers the brand's new "pay-to-play" mechanism.
- Brand communications have evolved from mass to personalized to peer-to-peer. Peer-to-peer media won't completely unseat traditional media.
- Each shopper is a brand.
- Shoppers advocate brands that align with their personal values and image.
- Each shopper is a media vehicle.
- Self-serve promotions: shoppers are assuming the labor of promoting the brand to themselves, in exchange for virtual currency and soft currency. In many cases, the sales associate is completely disintermediated.
- Interactive entertainment increases participation rates and is becoming a discipline in its own right, such as gamification.
- Do-it-yourself advocacy and pass-along promotions: shoppers are assuming the labor of brand communications.

The New Path to Purchase

WHAT IS THE PATH TO PURCHASE?

A few decades ago, consumer packaged goods (CPG) companies thought about their product introductions in these terms: awareness, trial, repeat (ATR). Consumers would become aware of a product, would be induced to try it, and (hopefully) would repeat their purchase, becoming a regular consumer of the item.

This thinking worked well in a predigital world. Awareness would come through several traditional media sources—television, print, radio, and outdoor. Ad agencies honed their craft, developing sophisticated methods for embedding brands in consumers' minds and memories. Here is a great proof point: Ronald McDonald is second only to Santa in terms of recognition. More than 96 percent of schoolchildren recognize Ronald McDonald, according to *Ad Age*.[1]

Next, a trial purchase took place in a store. Trade and promotion campaigns were refined and perfected, geared to induce shoppers to put a product in their basket. Repeat purchases would depend on the performance of the product, which had been thoroughly tested among consumers. While the ATR model was used for financial modeling purposes, it also served as a rough way to think about marketing holistically.

Over time, marketers began to embrace a more multifaceted approach that described the task of *shopping* very specifically. This shift was more fundamental and groundbreaking for marketing than it may seem. It was the shift from viewing the buyer as a *consumer* to viewing the buyer as a *shopper*.

What's the difference? A shopper is on a mission, or could be set on a mission, to buy something. Consumers are consuming something. Marketing efforts geared to shoppers are concerned first and foremost with the buying process rather than the consuming process. When CPG companies were strong and retailers were relatively weaker (a situation that is not so true now), brands could afford to focus on consumption behaviors such as use-up rates, in-home behaviors, awareness, and product performance, while pushing the problem of appealing to shoppers per se (in brick-and-mortar stores) onto their sales organizations, the trade, and promotion houses. At the time, these marketing functions were considered more tactical than strategic.

However, the picture changed. Retailers got scan data and became savvier in general. Trade and promotion houses saw their missions as extending well beyond the tactical, and they began to flex their muscles. TiVo and Hulu changed the dynamics of advertising and blunted the impact of some traditional campaign efforts. The stage was set for a new approach to marketing.

At this point, a new marketing model emerged that focused specifically on the tasks of shopping. The "funnel" paradigm of purchasing behavior, which began with awareness and ended in purchase (see Figure 3.1), was born. This early model helped sellers think about the buying process in a more refined way. For example, marketers could point to the discovery phase and create programs

---

Figure 3.1 | **Funnel Style Path to Purchase Model**

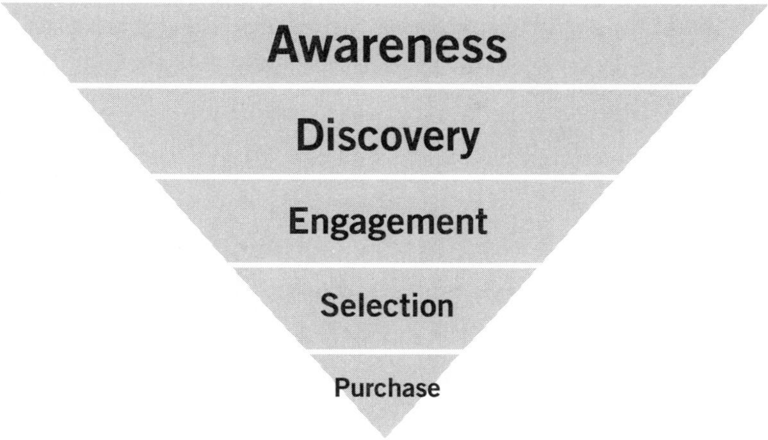

Awareness
Discovery
Engagement
Selection
Purchase

to aid the shopper in this specific task. The path to purchase paradigm helped to usher in the age of shopper marketing. According
to the 2008 glossary of the In-Store Marketing Institute (now the
Path-to-Purchase Institute), shopper marketing was defined as "*the
use of strategic insights into the shopper mindset to drive effective marketing and merchandising activity in a specific store environment.*"

THE NEW AGE OF SHOPPER MARKETING

Ultimately, digital technology antiquated the funnel model. There
are a few fundamental problems with this model. First, it is linear.
It begins with awareness and takes a straight line to purchase.

A linear path to purchase doesn't make sense in a digital
world. Shoppers get their information from a plethora of disparate
sources—traditional and digital, static and interactive, brand and
cohort. Online, a shopper may be investigating the benefits of a
brand, only to detour into an interactive educational module of a

competing brand. Or a long-planned purchase of, say, a national-brand sofa could be derailed by a friend sharing a Groupon for a local furniture store.

And shoppers are armed with entirely new capabilities as well. According to eMarketer, in May 2011, 36 percent of female shoppers use their mobile devices for price comparision. In the predigital age, price comparison was a laborious, time-consuming task that few shoppers would engage in extensively, except for higher-ticket items. The idea of "perfect information" in the marketplace was a theoretical concept taught in economics courses. Academics would speculate on how the market would behave under conditions of perfect information. Today, shoppers have all but perfect information—and a map of the nearest inventories to boot!

In response to digital technology, newer shapes for the path to purchase were brought forth. Now, there are wheels, matrices, spirals, clouds, and others. While a consensus as to the definitive shape has not been reached, nearly every shopper marketer agrees that the linear path to purchase has blown up.

New means of shopping demand an evolution of the model and a fresh definition of shopper marketing. Deloitte's Shopper Practice provides a holistic vision of shopper marketing that nicely accommodates digital shopping dynamics. In their seminal report with the Grocery Manufacturers Association (GMA) Deloitte defines shopper marketing this way: "All marketing stimuli, developed based on a deep understanding of shopper behavior, designed to build brand equity, engage the shopper (i.e., a consumer in 'shopping mode'), and lead him/her to a purchase."[2]

Thinking about shopper behaviors in terms of shopper currencies is most useful to marketers whose multiple objectives are to "build brand equity, engage the shopper, and lead him/her to a purchase." In other words, this book is geared to help the shopper marketer influence shoppers, using a behavior-for-scrip exchange concept.

MOMENTS OF TRUTH AND "STORE BACK"

Numerous articles have been written about Procter & Gamble's "First Moment of Truth" (FMOT). This phrase was coined to describe the moment when the shopper is standing in the aisle of a store, deciding whether to buy a particular item: either she puts it in her basket or she doesn't. It is a critical moment in the selling process.

This approach cast a new light on marketing, as many previous market research studies had indicated degrees of likelihood of buying on a five-point scale. But P&G knew that the reality was simpler—at that moment, either the shopper bought it or she didn't.

The second moment of truth is when the buyer uses the product and decides whether the product performs well enough to lead her to repeat the purchase. Product performance is critical to brand adoption.

The FMOT idea from P&G led to a reversal of the marketing process. Until FMOT, above-the-line ad agencies were responsible for developing a "big idea" and an ensuing television campaign (with accompanying radio, print, and outdoor messages). In-store communications simply followed suit. This was the "matching luggage" approach to mass marketing. However, FMOT changed that. The FMOT approach implied that the selling moment in the store was the first critical moment with the buyer. This meant that marketing ideas should start with this moment in mind. The marketing process was reconceived from the "store back."

P&G's Store Back concept was featured in *Shopper Marketing* magazine in 2010. That article reported, "'Store Back reorients our thinking as we're developing big ideas for our brands,' explains [P&G's] global design officer Phil Duncan. 'We're asking our brand teams to first really start with the store in mind as they evaluate their big ideas, because what we have found is we actually develop better big ideas if we think about the store first and work our way back.' This is a reversal of the way CPGs and their agencies have traditionally approached marketing campaigns, which meant starting with TV or print applications and then adapting them to fit the store."[3]

As digital shopping became pervasive and the recession hit most shoppers, a new phrase emerged, "the Zero Moment of Truth" (ZMOT). Google coined this phrase to point out that most shoppers were in fact searching for deals, discounts, and product information online *prior* to visiting the store to make a purchase.

According to Google's CPG blog (http://www.zeromoment oftruth.com/), data from IRI showed that 83 percent of shoppers had made their decision before entering the store.[4] The recession gave most shoppers an incentive to search for the best deal before burning gas to get to the store, and technology was giving them the means to do so. These preshopping search behaviors have become entrenched shopping behavior for many buyers.

Recently, I had a conversation with Catherine Roe, head of consumer packaged goods at Google. She commented about the change in shopping and search habits. "Consumers now have an ingrained habit of doing research prior to shopping; 76 percent of shoppers make a written or digital list before going to the store. Even as the recession subsides, shoppers now know they can find deals and make better shopping decisions by planning and incorporating this zero moment of truth into their shopping behavior.

"P&G didn't invent Shopper Marketing. They revitalized it in the modern age and led the rest of us to appreciate the beauty of the concept. Eighteen years ago, or so, while working to improve [what] was then a poor relationship between P&G and Walmart, P&G came to realize that collaborating with a retail partner in order to genuinely (and jointly) serve that chain's shoppers had an extraordinarily positive effect on sales (not to mention relations with that vital customer). In our view, the truths of shopper marketing are probably ancient. They were just obscured by fifty years of branding via mass media.

"P&G did introduce the concept that there are two Moments of Truth that have to be won to succeed in consumer product marketing. They actually boiled the whole proposition down to a simple poetic phrase: when she chooses and when she uses. Which is to say that the first objective is to get your product into the shopper's cart and then have it pass muster when consumed. While that notion is still valid, their definition of what constitutes a Moment of Truth has broadened significantly. For example, getting scribbled, with a specific mention of the brand, onto the shopper's shopping list is one of those moments, as is being researched and purchased on-line. Effectively influencing a myriad of touch-points along the path to purchase, both pre- and post-, (via search, video, social media, retail sites, and increasingly mobile, etc.) now vies with the last three feet in order of magnitude in the evolving science of shopper marketing." Peter Hoyt, Executive Director and CEO, Path to Purchase Institute, http://www.p2pi.org/.

I like to tell the story of my neighbor, who has four teenage boys and is not particularly tech-savvy. Historically, she says, she went to Jewel [a local grocery store] four to five times per week and was frustrated by her grocery bill and the amount the family spent eating out. The recession hit, and she started doing more research before hitting the store. She prints coupons, reads reviews, scours the online circulars, and, most important, plans her meals for the entire week. She now goes to Jewel once or twice per week, eats out much less, and says she's saving $200 to $250 per week by leveraging ZMOT (she doesn't call it that!). That's a vacation or college money, she says, and this is a habit that is now ingrained in her path to purchase.

THE PATH TO PURCHASE ENDS AT ADVOCACY

The path to purchase, store back, and ZMOT have been important steps forward in evolving marketing thinking. However, in practice, these approaches can still leave money on the table. The reason is that in many cases, marketing efforts actually end when the shopper buys . . . only to start all over again when her need arises again.

The money left on the table comes in the form of opportunity costs—the opportunity cost of selling without meaningful loyalty incentives, the opportunity cost of not building advocacy mechanisms into a sale, and the opportunity cost of failing to invest the shopper in a participatory process, outside of purchase. The digital world reroutes the path to purchase so that it is a path to advocacy (see Figure 3.2).

Participation, advocacy, and loyalty are often afterthoughts bolted onto a marketing program or brand idea. These objectives need to be fully built into a brand proposition and the financial

Figure 3.2 | **Shopping Cycle**

benchmarking of success. These shopper behaviors have financial value, which can enhance brand value and help ensure future revenue streams. Increasingly, the job of the shopper marketer will be to entrench these objectives—both strategic and financial—into marketing plans, alongside more traditional goals like purchase and penetration.

The next chapters will discuss the strategic uses of advocacy, loyalty, and participation. But before we dive into evaluating these shopper behaviors, it will be useful to blueprint a purchase-cycle model.

A PURCHASE MODEL FOR THE SHOPPER ECONOMY

While there are many purchase-cycle models out there, we have to settle on one to discuss in this book. Toward that end, I have synthesized a few ideas to create a streamlined and, I hope, commonsense approach to the shopping cycle.

It makes sense to organize the steps in a wheel shape to represent a cycle of shopping. Shopping is a repetitive process. Furthermore, advocacy and loyalty depend on the shopper's having a relationship with a brand, which also implies repeated engagement.

However, the steps may not always be sequential. For example, a traditional grocery shopper may navigate to her store and the product category, then evaluate brands at the shelf. On the other hand, ZMOT may be in effect, and the shopper could evaluate brands in a category before navigating to a purchase point (digital or conventional). Also, it's conceivable that a shopper might advocate a product that she hasn't tried yet. (I've actually spoken with bloggers who have done this.) So, while the wheel makes sense in a general way, the arrangement also means that the shopper can pivot through the hub of the wheel to any step, at any time.

The following are quick descriptors of each phase of the cycle.

Awareness

Awareness is a conventional starting point for a path to purchase—how can a shopper consider a brand she is not aware of? That is true, but sometimes this is a dormant phase. Awareness itself does not always prompt action. Brand loyalists may have the brand so embedded in their lives that, in the absence of product news, becoming aware isn't an activity.

On the other hand, in a digital space, when awareness is a reminder, it can lead to purchase because of the immediacy of buying options available to the shopper. Examples here include text alerts and mobile in-store promotions.

Consideration

Consideration is the starting point for action in this cycle. (Sometimes a trigger or prompt step is broken out separately.) The shopper becomes mentally, emotionally, and ultimately logistically engaged in considering whether to buy a brand. The consideration set is the set of brands that a shopper feels is within his personal circle of possibilities.

This phase can occur almost anywhere, with or without a follow-up purchase. Consideration and evaluation can occur on a laptop, on an iPad, on a mobile phone, at an event, with a friend, or, soon, on interactive television. Here consideration is the shopper's response to an effective message that sparks a desire, then presents an immediate opportunity to pursue that desire. Taken further, consideration becomes evaluation—weighing the pros and cons of a product or brand relative to the alternatives.

Evaluation

Evaluation is carried out by shoppers who are new to the category and those who are confronted with new options (flavors, prices, sizes, or brands). More often than not, CPG shoppers are not actively evaluating *everything* that they put into their baskets, whether online or in the physical store. Buying certain brands and products can be a habit, a preference, or a mission. Evaluation, especially for a brand loyalist, may be a dormant part of the shopper's purchase cycle for that category. For these brand loyalists, consideration may be just inclusion on the shopping list and evaluation may be dormant.

Again, this step may not be sequential. The shopper may have researched and found a product in the ZMOT, only to reconsider and reevaluate options at the shelf.

Navigation

Navigation is the next step. In this phase, the shopper is endeavoring to find the product and the means to purchase it. This could be online, on the mobile, in a brick-and-mortar store, through a friend, on Groupon, or through a combination of these. Identifying where to buy a product (as well as where it may be located within that environment) is a step with its own set of considerations for the shopper. Again, this step can occur "out of order"— for example, before consideration.

Selection and Purchase

Selection and purchase have been combined into one step in this cycle. This is the moment when a shopper selects a product with the intention of buying it. In a physical store, the purchase may be considered done, in the shopper's mind, when the item hits the trolley. In fact, in Stop & Shop stores, shoppers can scan the product when they pick it up from the shelf and before they drop it in the cart. All of the items in their cart are already on the bill.

Online, the purchase isn't complete until the shopper hits the confirmation button. Shopping cart abandonment is a much more widespread phenomenon online than it is in brick-and-mortar stores (it does happen in traditional stores, but the percentage is much lower).

Consumption and advocacy are broken into two separate phases here.

Consumption

Consumption includes usage, gifting, storage, disposal, and memories. The brand experience is consumed, and any aftermath impressions are a part of that. Examples of consumption memories could look like this: "We love the frozen pizza, but the box won't fit in our freezer." Or, "I liked the new shampoo, but my husband really loved the smell."

Advocacy

Advocacy should be a phase in every marketer's purchase model. Liking a brand, reviewing or rating a retailer or product, and even just sharing coupons should be part of engaging the shopper after consumption in order to help solidify the relationship with the buyer. Advocacy is the final step on the new path to purchase.

INTERVIEW WITH KEN BARNETT, CEO, MARS ADVERTISING

Shopper marketing organizations have been on the front lines of the changing marketplace. To discuss the evolving nature of reaching shoppers and the impact on organizing agency talent, I talked to Ken Barnett. Ken is the CEO of MARS Advertising, which is distinguished as a four-time winner of the Hub Top 12 Shopper Marketing Agencies.

Q: Today, shoppers can access information about brand benefits, product reviews, prices, and fellow buyers, and also access opportunities to purchase on the spot. In this environment, how do brands sabotage themselves or set themselves up for success?

A: *The ubiquity of information has meant that, over time, our influencers have changed. In the 1960s and 1970s, Mr. Whipple and Marcus Welby were influencers. Consumers perceived these characters as being "people I know" and "professionals." They influenced purchase decisions. Today, consumers choose their own influencers, and for the most part these people are more authentic than Mr. Whipple. The power of influence is entrusted to retailers (such as Best Buy or Sears), friends and family (via social networks and word of mouth), and other digital points of entry (reviewer sites like Yelp, brand websites, and so on). Shoppers can pick and choose who will be educating, inspiring, and incenting them.*

Unfortunately, this system has reopened the old world of payola radio, where DJs were paid to identify the songs they played as "hits." Ratings and reviews that are written by brand employees or paid advocates compromise the integrity of today's influence system. While this kind of sabotage isn't universal, there are notable examples, such as the hotel industry, which has been caught gaming the system. What matters here is lying about the review—not that the reviewer is paid.

To succeed, brands and retailers need real transparency. The authenticity of the reviewer is crucial in today's influence system.

During a recent presentation, Bill Simon, the CEO of Walmart, said that if you go back to the beginning of time, wherever two rivers intersected, you always had a merchant environment. This phenomenon will continue to exist even as the two rivers become digital intersections of traffic. I agree with this statement.

Brick-and-mortar merchants have integrated digital media in many convenient and clever ways, such as site-to-store buying. However, there is a problem in certain higher-ticket, investigation-intensive categories, like electronics, home appliances, and flooring. Retailers such as Best Buy are becoming showrooms for the Internet. The Blue Shirt educates the shopper in-store, where he or she touches and sees the product. Then the shopper consults his or her mobile phone for competitive pricing and availability. In many cases, the shopper buys from a competing retailer without even leaving the store! In a very real sense, this is stealing.

What's the quid pro quo for the product education? If I go into Store A to be educated, and then take that information to buy from Store B, is that fair? What's that worth?

> *LIZ: Ken asks a good question. How do we recapture the value of educating shoppers, or prevent competitive sales resulting from educating shoppers? Part of the answer may lie in the technology itself. Shoppers need to be identified while they are seeking information—either in-store or online—before they buy. GPS and cookies may help with this. Then there is an opportunity to give them incentives to buy from the educator, effectively undercutting interlopers. The level of information sought could work as a mechanism to qualify shoppers, thus reducing the "waste" in educating those who are unlikely to buy.*

Q: Given all of these changes, what is the role of the agency now?

A: *The role the agency is morphing radically. This was summarized in an article called "Future Shock," published in the* HUB *Magazine in 2011.*

The marketing timeline is being turned on its head. The retailer is setting the timeline for marketing. Retailers need a 12- to 18-month lead time to prepare for a brand shopping experience. There is some irony in this conflict. The brand says, "The retailer never executes properly." The retailer says, "The brand never gives us enough time!" The simple solution is to incorporate the operations team more effectively, and to allow enough time up front.

But the implications of this may be uncomfortable for some agencies. It means that the ad agency needs to execute against the shopper marketer brief. The reason is that speed to broadcast messages is faster than speed to brick-and-mortar experiences. To align them properly means to put the experience development before the communication.

Q: Shopper behaviors are becoming increasingly important in the digital environment, where messages can be shared and reshared en masse. Do you have an example of a brand that is a leader in partnering with shoppers?

A: *We were privileged to work with Colgate on a wonderful educational campaign called the "Invisible Nasties." We learned that people took the cleanliness of their toothbrush for granted. Unfortunately, it's not as clean as consumers believe. It's kept after sickness, and it is kept in a location that invites germs of all kinds. The campaign sought to educate people that their toothbrush must be changed every three months. The way we did this was through social media.*

Q: Shoppers are experiencing brands in new ways and in new contexts, including mobile, augmented reality, omnipresent social graph, and so on. These changes mean that branded experiences are morphing dramatically. How should agencies respond, in terms of talent recruitment and team structure?

A: *Time was, you hired a television team for a big client, and the creative people were identified by discipline. But no more! It's a mistake to think this way today. Because there are so many ways to communicate and create experiences, it is more important than ever that creative teams service the brand, not pander to the technology. Furthermore, the client doesn't want yet another handoff to yet another agency or team. The creative team needs to use all media, integrating the talent within the team to meet objectives. You can have specialists and visionaries, but you need to know the brand first and best to succeed.*

CHAPTER 3 Recap: *The New Path to Purchase*

- Marketers have shifted from viewing the buyer as a *consumer* to viewing the buyer as a *shopper*. Shopper marketing examines the tasks of *shopping* very specifically, in order to influence behavior at each step of the decision-making and acquisition process.

- Shopper marketing includes "All marketing stimuli, developed based on a deep understanding of shopper behavior, designed to build brand equity, engage the shopper (i.e., a consumer in 'shopping mode'), and lead him/her to a purchase."[5]

  - The path to purchase is a marketing model that focuses specifically on the tasks of shopping, from the shopper's perspective.

  - "First Moment of Truth" (FMOT) is P&G's idea that the shopper standing at the shelf either will or will not put the product in the basket.

  - "Store Back" is the marketing process that results when the shopper's decision at the shelf is considered first and other brand communications flow from the store back.

  - "Zero Moment of Truth" (ZMOT) is Google's perspective that most shoppers preshop online before actually purchasing.

- The traditional path to purchase has changed in a digital age, because the path is no longer linear and its destination may be not purchase, but advocacy.

  - Omitting advocacy, loyalty, and participation from a purchase model leaves money on the table, in terms of opportunity costs.

- The shopper economy purchase-cycle model (see Figure 3.3).

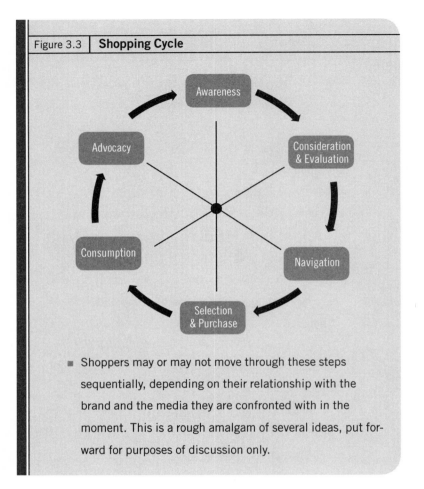

Figure 3.3 | **Shopping Cycle**

- Shoppers may or may not move through these steps sequentially, depending on their relationship with the brand and the media they are confronted with in the moment. This is a rough amalgam of several ideas, put forward for purposes of discussion only.

4

Around the Wheel

SETTING STRATEGY

So far, we've seen that in many cases, shoppers are performing the labor of marketing. The exchange value of shopper currency is incentive enough to push the shopper around the purchase cycle (see Figure 4.1). Shoppers are using less out-of-pocket cash and more of their own labor. Especially in a recession, this seems like a good deal to many shoppers. And it's a good deal for marketers, too. Commissioning the shoppers directly can mean effective, profitable programming.

Pushing the Purchase Cycle with Shopper Currency

Throughout the purchase cycle, specific marketing objectives can be achieved with shopper currencies. By giving potential buyers incentives to pay attention, the marketer gains awareness among a new group of users. Also, current buyers can be made aware of news. Compensating shoppers directly is part of the budget for the campaign. Right now this may not have the magnitude of the

---

| Figure 4.1 | **Pushing the Purchase Cycle with Shopper Currency** |

Attention

Advocacy   Advocacy   Awareness

                Loyalty
                The Ghost in   Consideration
Consumption   the Machine   & Evaluation

                                            Participation

        Selection   Navigation
        & Purchase

Hard Currency

---

reach of television, but message delivery is more assured, and the possibilities for targeting may be more assured as well.

Paying for attention may also gain the marketer consideration. If a message is delivered to the right buyer in a timely fashion, that buyer may internalize a call to action or reevaluate his brand choices. This is what traditional advertising has been doing for years. The only difference here is that the shopper is being compensated directly and personally.

How does search engine optimization (SEO) fit in? Product search is an important part of the shopping path. Grabbing a shopper's attention and awareness early in the search process is often an important (and even vital) part of completing a sale. However, it isn't shopper currency unless the searcher is *earning* scrip. As of this writing, there is a program that lets shoppers earn scrip for searching. Bing has a program that rewards shoppers for searching using its engine. Bing's virtual currency offers exchange rates with several other virtual brand currencies, including those at Facebook, Starbucks, and FarmVille, among others.

Participation covers a lot of territory, but basically it includes any shopper action other than simple attention, hard cash purchase, or advocacy. This is principally where gamification fits into the marketing mix. Shoppers are motivated to participate when interaction is set up in a gamelike paradigm. Gabe Zichermann, gamification guru, says that consumers will work for SAPS. "SAPS is an acronym that stands for status, access, power, and stuff. Simply put it is a system of rewards. Conveniently, it lists each potential prize in order from the most to the least desired, the most sticky to the least sticky, and the cheapest to the most expensive."[1]

But what does the marketer get out of it? Participation goals should be carefully thought out. It's possible to have shoppers getting rewarded for activities that don't push them around the purchase cycle. This is the activity-for-activity's-sake pitfall. Bearing this in mind, participation *can* do a few things very well—for example, it can keep the brand top of mind during consideration (in turn driving trial or frequency). It can communicate a brand personality through interaction, or it can convert buyers during their evaluation period, then give them an incentive for purchase. We'll be looking at some examples of this later. Participation can also fuel other marketing assets, such as advocacy and loyalty.

Using virtual currency to give shoppers incentives for advocacy is commonplace now. This is a great strategy for recruiting new users and increasing the base, especially when the product is obscure or a hard sell. Peer-to-peer advocacy is twice as effective as brand-to-consumer messaging. A recommendation, coupon, or positive review from a friend is much more likely to convince a new user to try a new restaurant, movie, brand of electronics, hotel, hairdresser, or plumber. These are higher-ticket, higher-involvement categories than typical consumer packaged goods (CPGs). However, recommending a fast-moving-goods program to a friend can also work. Because most CPGs are lower-involvement, incentives for advocacy often involve donations to charitable causes (breast cancer, local schools, and so on). For example, in July 2010 Procter & Gamble (P&G) offered to donate $1 to the Special Olympics for every "like" on Facebook. This is a way in which groups of friends can spread the word to one another and contribute to a good cause, all sponsored by P&G, which gets the halo. P&G is being advocated, but in this case, as the sponsor of a good cause.[2]

Loyalty is the ghost in the machine. *Genuine* loyalty is brand commitment, which transcends simple intent to buy. It is the alignment of a buyer's self-image with the brand equity.

Loyal users are often the most profitable segment of the brand's revenue stream. The loyal customer's lifetime value (CLV) is higher than that of others. We'll address some examples of radical alignment and loyalty, as well as how rabid loyalists don't need additional compensation for their devotion. However, the focus here will be on the more pedestrian *what's-it-in-for-me* mindset, which means loyalty programs. In the context of shopper currency, loyalty means an intent or commitment to buy in the future.

BARRIERS AND MOTIVATORS

Shopper marketers need to think about what hurdles might prevent a shopper from buying a brand. While this may seem like a negative approach, helping the shopper overcome hurdles makes for good strategy. Although impediments to purchasing any particular product can be quite detailed, this is a general list of impediments to purchase.

- Awareness: I've never heard of the product.

- Location: I don't know where or how to find the product.

- Relevance: The product isn't for me. I don't need it.

- Price-value: It isn't worth the price.
    - Use: I don't know how to use the product. It is confusing.

- Believability: I don't believe the product claims.

Getting the shopper to expend effort is similar to getting her to spend dollars. Hurdles must be overcome. In the case of spending shopper currency (APAL behaviors), the obstacles are slightly modified. Let's look at the use of a mobile social network as a participation program, simply to illustrate how these criteria might yield communications priorities.

- Awareness: I've never heard of this mobile social network.

- Location: I don't know how to access this mobile social network.

- Relevance: I don't think the network is relevant to me. It is for other people.

- Price-value: I don't think it's worth the effort. The rewards are insufficient. Or I don't believe the rewards that are being touted.
    - Use: I don't know how to use it. It is too hard to use.

- Security: I am nervous about surrendering my personal information to this company.

- Social status: I might look like a fool if I used this platform.

Looking at a shopper currency program from the perspective of this list can help develop strategy. For example, if we knew that lack of awareness was preventing shoppers from participating in the program, we could launch a campaign to tell the world about it. Location is less of an issue in the digital space because shoppers and consumers of media know that they can access almost anything through a search engine.

Relevance may be more of an issue for specialty or targeted programs. Thus, for example, earning points for a local school district by scanning products may feel irrelevant to someone who has no children. In terms of spending time and effort, targeting is paramount for achieving relevance.

Price-value is one of the biggest obstacles to spending any shopper currency. Since a shopper's time and energy are finite, spending these resources is a zero-sum game. Opportunity costs are weighed heavily. Difficulty or ease of use can make or break programs. The reason "use" is listed as a subordinate bullet under price-value is that an increase in difficulty requires an increase in time and effort, effectively changing the value equation. Any shopper labor must be worth the effort.

Behavior-based programs in a digital space carry the burden of establishing trust among their participants. Users must feel assured that their private information won't be shared in ways that they are uncomfortable with, and that their information won't be hacked and stolen. Even for an attention currency, the shopper needs to feel assured that opting in will be safe and worthwhile, and that exiting, if desired, will be easy. While security is a barrier to shopper currency, it is not a hurdle that has normally been listed as a barrier to purchasing from the retailer, per se. However, in the digital space, retailer security is increasingly emerging as a hurdle.

Many retailers will ask the buyer if they wish to "check in" using social media, typically their Facebook account. This has nothing but upside for the seller, who can gain access to the shopper's basic information (picture, gender, list of friends, likes, birthday, hometown, and so on), e-mail account, wall (including access to posting), and personal network (friends and friends' information, like their birthdays, likes, activities, hometowns, and so on). While some shoppers are reluctant to surrender their social media access, other shoppers may be unwilling even to create a simple account with the seller. These shoppers are concerned about how and when the retailer may contact them in the future or use their personal information. Online retailers who don't wish to lose a sale to a skittish customer let shoppers check out as "guests." Even though shoppers are encouraged to create an account or to check in using social media, the option to simply buy on a one-off basis usually exists to overcome the "security" hurdle.

Finally, social status is a real issue in the digital space. At the very least, participants must feel that their reputations won't be harmed if they participate in brand activities. The perception that they would be sacrificing some social capital would be a real impediment to many. On the other hand, enhanced social status is an incentive to participate and/or advocate. To some extent, the social status barrier is also a purchase barrier, but less so, since it is fairly easy to hide one's actual purchases (for example, hemorrhoid cream can be kept hidden in a bathroom drawer).

ATTENTION PROGRAMS—ACHIEVING AWARENESS AND LIFT

Sears has done a terrific job with its digital marketing, bundling several ways to engage with the brand. Sticking with the currency of attention (see Figure 4.2) for this example, Sears launched *Ad-YourWay*, a digital advertising program that had an enticing prem-

Figure 4.2	Attention		
Shopper Currency	**Impedes Behavior**	**Motivates Behavior**	**Marketer's Gain**
Attention	• Negative price-value • Consumes my time and attention without sufficient reward • Irrelevant • Security issues	• Relevant value • Timeliness • Convenience • Entertainment	• Awareness • Consideration • Lift

ise: personalized ads and offers on your mobile. According to the website, "AdYourWay is a revolutionary new tool that gets to know you and personalizes the shopping offers you receive." There have been personalized ads already available, including those customized ads that pop up during regular "surfing" sessions. But this is a little different, because shoppers can opt in to brand messages in order to get personalized value. In particular, shoppers can find an item that they would like to buy, then enter the price point they are willing to pay. AdYourWay notifies the shopper when the item becomes available at that price. This is similar to a buyout auction. The attention that the shopper is willing to pay is in exchange for the value of the notice. Furthermore, if the shopper buys, she can get "Shop Your Way" reward points.

Sears is offering shoppers messages in exchange for value in its stores. The messages themselves are a kind of reminder advertising for the retailer, driving lift every time they break. However, there are some attention-for-value mechanisms that are separated from the shopper's regular purchase cycle. An example of this is Varolo. com.[3] Varolo is a website where consumers can sign up to watch ads in exchange for a cash reward and chances in a lottery. Advertisers are literally giving the audience members part of the media budget in exchange for their attention. Interestingly, Varolo has created a financial incentive for viewers to invite friends to join Varolo: the viewer gets a percentage of his friends' earnings. It's a profit-sharing scheme using a social network. Viewers can create a "village" of viewers who earn wages for watching ads. Viewers earn compensation from "friends' friends" up to three and four degrees of separation (friends' friends' friends—like a pyramid). However, in the case of Varolo, the viewers are media consumers who are working for wages, not necessarily in connection with their shopping cycle. The motive here is the wage (which is heavily emphasized), rather than a specific shopper advantage like the one that Sears offers.

While Varolo (or even Facebook) attention schemes are a new way of delivering "above-the-line" video advertising, I am not sure that they are as effective for the shopper marketer. The reason is that media consumers for hire are not as immediately immersed in their shopping cycle. Retailer reminder ads carry specific incentives to shop, whereas Varolo and Facebook Credit ads are messages whose incentive is either virtual or hard currency (not usually direct discounts on goods). While this is true at this writing, there may come a time when above-the-line ads may be watched for virtual currency in a *purchase-cycle context*. However, I am not sure that this has been well done yet. I suspect that we will see this happen when web-enabled television becomes more widespread and sophisticated.

PARTICIPATION PROGRAMS—GAINING CONSIDERATION AND NEW USERS

Participation programs (see Figure 4.3) sometimes flounder because the time and effort are not worth the reward, or because the redemption is too difficult. For example, in the predigital era, the "Labels for Education" program was launched. Shoppers could clip UPC codes from participating products, mail them to a processing center, and then get a certain number of points that could

Figure 4.3	Participation		
Shopper Currency	**Impedes Behavior**	**Motivates Behavior**	**Marketer's Gain**
Participation	• Negative price-value • Consumes my time and effort without sufficient reward • Irrelevant • Security issues	• Entertainment • Simplicity • Convenience Rewards per Zichermann: • Status • Access • Power • Stuff	• Consideration • New users • Involvement/ engagement "Social status" of numbers of participants

be used to benefit their local schools. This was a very worthy and popular program. However, once the Internet and frequent shopper cards became ubiquitous, the program was improved and supplemented. Under Campbell's "eLabels for Education" Program, shoppers register their shopper card (with a participating retailer) online, designate the school they would like to donate to, and then simply "shop, swipe, and earn." Since time and effort are part of the shopper's value equation for participating, this was a big step forward in making this worthwhile program convenient. In fact, participation rates improved dramatically after the launch of the eLabels program.

I am putting this program into the participation bucket rather than the loyalty bucket because shoppers are really showing loyalty to their local schools and to the eLabels program rather than to a particular brand. But brands do benefit. Brands are getting trial from shoppers who might not have considered purchasing their product (in order to get the points for the school). Brands are also getting pantry-loading behavior from loyal buyers. Also, there is the halo effect of the charitable donation as well.

Charitable donations are a powerful motivator to the right audience, especially during times of economic recession. Using these kinds of programs, shoppers can give to the cause of their choice, without necessarily parting with cash. The recession of

2007 spurred the acceptance of all manner of scrip because shoppers were short of cash. Shoppers were eager to embrace alternative means to earn value; in 2009, even simple coupon redemption jumped 27 percent, the highest increase in 17 years.[4]

Mobile social media are great mechanisms for participation programming. Foursquare has been used as a participation program by several national brands, including Pepsi, Chili's, and American Express. Continuing with the charitable donation examples, Pepsi urged foursquare participants to check in, using donations to a cause as an incentive.

Is it worth it? According to an article in *Nation's Restaurant News*, foursquare has more than 2 million users and adds 100,000 users a week. With this in mind, Chili's created a traffic-driving program with the location-based social network in the summer of 2010. Foursquare users needed only to check into a local Chili's and show the waiter their mobile to receive free chips and salsa. Waiters were instructed to record a code for each redemption.

This is a great example of a national chain driving store traffic in exchange for shopper value. *NRN* reported that Stacey Sullivan, a spokesperson for Chili's parent, said, "The chain is seeing a 20-percent redemption rate among those checking in and redeeming their actions for the chips and salsa. 'We're seeing excellent results on the campaign,' she said. 'Guests are very excited. Every week since the foursquare offer began, the number of check-ins has doubled.'"[5]

From the shopper's perspective, the redemption was simple, the reward valuable, and the participation fun. From the marketer's perspective, the offer drove traffic. This kind of program can bring in new users and lapsed users, and increase the frequency of regulars. While this example is from foursquare, there are several other mobile social networks available that can offer similar marketing opportunities, including Loopt, Gowalla, and Brightkite, to name a few.

LOYALTY PROGRAMS—INCREASING THE LIFETIME VALUE OF CUSTOMERS AND PROFITABILITY

The goal of most loyalty programs (see Figure 4.4) is the same—to capture a great percentage of the shopper's share of wallet for the category. The share of requirements (SOR) is the number of brand purchases divided by the number of purchases in that category. This is a calculation for an individual shopper. As a practical matter (at least until now), the share of requirements metric was most often used with a segment of shoppers.[6] So, for example, loyal users in some categories may buy Brand X on average for 40 percent of their total requirements, while in another category, loyalists may buy Brand Y for 80 percent of their total requirements. Normal SOR percentages vary by category. Loyalty programs can also provide incentives for increased frequency of purchasing, usage rates, cross-selling, and upselling. Share of wallet, frequency, and complementary-purchase consideration can become entrenched habits with a good shopper points program.

In many loyalty programs, the brand reimburses a small percentage of the loyalist's purchases in exchange for a steady (and hopefully larger than average) stream of revenue. Making sure this

Figure 4.4	**Loyalty**		
Shopper Currency	**Impedes Behavior**	**Motivates Behavior**	**Marketer's Gain**
Loyalty	• Consumes share of wallet without sufficient reward • Cumbersome (poor price-value of shopper's effort) • Irrelevant (infrequent shopper) • Security issues	• Perceived worth of rewards • Simplicity of earning • Simplicity of redemption • Frequency of rewards (for lesser-value programming)	• Increased lifetime value of shopper (share of wallet usage rates, upselling, etc.) • Involvement/ engagement

equation stays in the black can be a challenge for many brands. Later chapters address the financial aspects of incentives for shopper currency, including loyalty.

Since all of us have had experience with these programs in one form or another, I'll just look at two examples. American Express Membership Rewards is an outstanding loyalty program because of its longevity, access to a host of sellers, and ease of use (pay, earn, redeem). In terms of overcoming hurdles, anyone using an Amex card can easily participate without extra steps. The company also has a terrific reputation for helping to settle disputes between sellers and buyers, often advocating for the shopper. This reputation, coupled with pro-buyer theft and fraud policies, helps to overcome any security concerns on the part of the shopper. Rewards are generous and flexible: cash cards, gift cards, airline and hotel points, charitable donations, gifting—the list goes on. Amex users accrue points simply and can redeem them easily in a multitude of ways. The company's slogan epitomizes its loyalty objective: Don't Leave Home Without It.

On the other hand, there is the cumbersome My Starbucks Rewards program. As of this writing, loyalists must acquire a Starbucks card and load it with money, using cash, debit, or credit from another monetary source. The buyer must then register the card online with Starbucks. Rewards are earned whenever the buyer purchases an item at Starbucks using the "loaded" card. The shopper has to keep reloading the card with money and reusing the card to earn "stars." Shoppers earn one star every time they pay with the card.

Now there are two levels of rewards for stars: Green and Gold. The shopper earns Green level rewards after five stars. The Green level entitles the shopper to free syrups and milk, free refills, and a beverage with any purchase of a one-pound bag of coffee. (Not long ago, *anyone* buying a bag of coffee automatically got a free drink.) Gold level rewards kick in after 30 stars. Gold rewards include a free drink after every 15 swipes.

What are the hindrances to participating in this program? The effort of loading, reloading, and paying is a hassle. I have stood in line with 30 anxious, gotta-get-to-work patrons behind me, waiting to have the clerk reload my Starbucks card from my debit card and then pay for the goods.

There are three things Starbucks needs to do here to make this program work. It needs to increase the

1. Perceived value of rewards (Absolute level of frequency)

2. Simplicity of earning

3. Simplicity of redemption

Sure, some Starbucks lovers run this gauntlet. And sure, other buyers will be loyal to the franchise regardless. Even so, I believe the My Starbucks Rewards program isn't achieving its potential because as of now, it is tailored for the convenience of the seller rather than the buyer.

ADVOCACY PROGRAMS—CONVERTING NEW USERS AND CREATING RELATIONSHIPS

There are several motivators behind brand advocacy (see Figure 4.5). In June of 2011, David Aaker, vice chairman of Prophet and the author of *Brand Relevance: Making Competitors Irrelevant*, wrote a blog entry entitled, "Secrets of Social Media Revealed 50 Years Ago." The article was about Ernst Dichter's research on word of mouth, published in the *Harvard Business Review* in 1966.

Figure 4.5	**Advocacy**		
Shopper Currency	**Impedes Behavior**	**Motivates Behavior**	**Marketer's Gain**
Advocacy	• Consumes social capital without sufficient reward • Embarrassing • Cumbersome (price-value of effort) • Security issues	• Enhanced social status -Affiliation or superiority • Perceived value of reward (virtual incentives, etc.) • Altruism—helping others	• Converting new users • Profitability • Creating and enhancing customer relationships • Expanded (virtual) product offering

Dichter identified four reasons that a person would communicate about brands.

> The first (about 33% of the cases) is because of product-involvement. The experience is so novel and pleasurable that it must be shared. The second (about 24%) is self-involvement. Sharing knowledge or opinions is a way to gain attention, show connoisseurship, feel like a pioneer, have inside information, seek confirmation of a person's own judgment, or assert superiority. The third (around 20%) is other-involvement. The speaker wants to reach out and help to express neighborliness, caring, and friendship. The fourth (around 20%) is message-involvement. The message is so humorous or informative that it deserves sharing.[7]

This was a badly needed acknowledgment that the word-of-mouth mechanism isn't new to marketers and that many of the motivators are the same. I would venture that the first and last reasons (pleasurable and humorous) are actually about self-involvement. If the sharer feels that the experience or message "must be" shared, the benefits of doing so are emotional or psychological. To

me, this means that the sharer perceives either that her relationships with others will be enhanced by sharing this message, or that
her personal status will be enhanced (as in the second motivator).
In either case, the incentive to share is driven by social status. The
desire to share in order to help others is altruism. For example, if
my nephew has a medical problem, I can send his parents a link on
the latest research. Even under these conditions, social self-interest
lurks nearby.

Another relatively new inducement to sharing is financial
incentives. These can come in the form of virtual currency. For
example, Sears has linked its loyalty program rewards, "Shop Your
Way" points, with participation activities in the MySears community. Here is a partial list of rewarded activities: uploading a profile
photo (500 points), writing a first product review (500 points),
getting a "read," that is, someone reads your review (25 points for
every 250 reads), and so on.[8] In other words, sharing in the social
network earns the participant virtual currency that is redeemable
for "real-world" goods at Sears. Dichter couldn't have foreseen this
in 1966!

While there are a number of incentives to share product information, there are barriers too. Putting aside security issues as "table
stakes," shoppers are hindered from sharing if the reward isn't
worth their time, effort, or social capital. Who wants to go out on
a limb to endorse a brand if the product is trivial (you gotta buy
these paper clips!) or has a shady history (fen-phen). It isn't worth
one's personal reputation.

On the other hand, there is the person who can't say no. If
a person spends his social clout on everything, then it will be valued less by a reader who knows that. In the digital realm, it is possible not to know the extent of a sharer's endorsements. However,
in any given social network, it may be relatively easy to identify
"brand tramps."

A fairly unique barrier here is the embarrassment factor. If using a product is inherently socially shameful, advocacy is almost out of the question. Here's what I mean: herpes medicine, adult diapers, and food stamps. There have been examples of celebrities who have tried to "socialize" categories with stigmas—Bob Dole for erectile dysfunction and Whoopi Goldberg for bladder leakage. But these examples prove the point: most ordinary folk wouldn't like to admit to the 400 people in their social network that they need adult diapers.

Cottonelle is an example of a brand that didn't address its social stigma hurdles adequately in a recent advocacy promotion. The Cottonelle "Getting Fresh with a Friend" campaign offers a $1.00 coupon for a tub of Cottonelle Flushable Moist Wipes in exchange for sharing your endorsement of the brand with a friend. There is a video of the "getting fresh" idea on its website, in addition to ads on television.

Here are a few viral Twitter feeds supplied by the brand for sharers to use on their social networks:

- Have you received a coupon for $1 off a tub of #CottonelleFreshFlushableMoistWipes? http://www.getfreshwithafriend.com
    - 2:00 PM Jul 05th from Cottonelle

- Have the Freshest of Fourths, friends.
    - 2:00 PM Jul 04th from Cottonelle

- Happy holiday weekend, everyone—stay #Fresh!
    - 2:00 PM Jul 01st from Cottonelle[9]

A program like this has almost nothing to lose and everything to gain from an advocacy program. However, while a number of women may have participated in this deal, I believe the embarrassment factor hasn't been properly addressed. Take a look at the painful video on Cottonelle's site. Perhaps it is meant to be funny or ironic, but the video also shows how awkward the company's treatment of the category is.

On the other hand, Poise, the brand that helps women control their light bladder leakage, has done a great job of addressing this barrier. The brand tackles it head on. Here's an excerpt from the Poise.com website. There is an incentive to share, but an altruistic one.

> *Did you know 1 in 3 of us has Light Bladder Leakage (LBL)? Many can benefit from your experiences.*
>
> *Share your story and let other women know about the life you're living, little leaks and all.*
>
> *As a thank you, we'll donate $1 in support of the <u>Women's Health Foundation</u> (up to $50,000).*
>
> And just to show good faith—
>
> *Not ready to share but want to show your support?*
>
> *No worries. Hit the link below and we'll still donate $1 towards the <u>Women's Health Foundation</u> (up to $50,000).*[10]

The point is that the best advocacy programming may gain a number of enthusiastic new category users, but sharing may still be restrained in categories with a social stigma.

The Groupon competitor LivingSocial has a well-designed advocacy program. It offers local group deals and a number of ways to share. In addition to links such as "send as a gift," "share on Facebook," and "tweet," LivingSocial posts a special offer with every deal. "Want it for free? Buy first, then share a special link. If three friends buy, yours is free!"[11] This program works because ordinary sharing (Facebook and Twitter) is offered, but the "freebie" is earned when others buy. This psychographic is clearly a bargain-hunting group. Offering its members a way to leverage its network to get something that is personally valuable is very motivating to shoppers and profitable for business.

Finally, brand advocacy can come in the form of virtual gifting. This may seem a little strange, but it works for some categories. A virtual gift is a digital representation of a "real-world" present, typically flowers, money, chocolates, "Best Dad" certificates, puppies and kittens, and other such items. Shoppers pay legal tender for virtual gifts. In fact, according to Ravi Mehta, a virtual goods insider, "Facebook, in particular, was criticized for gouging its users when it launched its Facebook Gifts program in February 2007, and many predicted that the program would be a dismal failure. During its first year, Facebook Gifts generated an estimated $15 million, or 10% of Facebook's overall $150 million in revenue for 2007."[12]

How do virtual gifts work with brand advocacy? Some savvy brands are offering virtual gifts as goods to "pass along" to friends and family. In other words, some brands are supplying branded virtual goods to use as "gifts." A virtual gift can be a simple icon (like a champagne glass) to bring a smile to the recipient. Or a branded gift, geared to be passed along, can be virtual currency like Facebook Credits, in-game credits, or even printable coupons. The point is that these gifts can provide an incentive to advocate. I imagine that shoppers may like some of them so much that they may be willing to pay fiat currency for them, turning advocacy tools into a profit center for the brand.

CHAPTER 4 Recap: *Around the Wheel*

- Specific marketing objectives can be achieved throughout the purchase cycle with shopper currencies (see Figure 4.6).
- Getting the shopper to expend effort is similar to getting her to spend dollars. Hurdles must be overcome. In the case of spending shopper currency (APAL behaviors), there are six basic hurdles:

    1. Awareness: I've never heard of this platform.
    2. Location: I don't know how to access this platform.
    3. Relevance: I don't think this platform is relevant to me. It is for other people.
    4. Price-value: I don't think it's worth the effort. The rewards are insufficient.
        - Use: I don't know how to use it. It is too hard to use.
    5. Security: I am nervous about surrendering my personal information to this company.
    6. Social status: I might look like a fool if I use this platform.

Figure 4.6	**Shopper Currency Barriers and Motivators**

Shopper Currency	Impedes Behavior	Motivates Behavior	Marketer's Gain
Attention	• Negative price-value • Consumes my time and attention without sufficient reward • Irrelevant • Security issues	• Relevant value • Timeliness • Convenience • Entertainment	• Awareness • Consideration • Lift
Participation	• Negative price-value • Consumes my time and effort without sufficient reward • Cumbersome • Boring • Irrelevant • Security issues	• Entertainment • Simplicity • Convenience Rewards per Zichermann: • Status • Access • Power • Stuff	• Consideration • New users • Involvement/ engagement • "Social status" of numbers of participants
Loyalty	• Consumes share of requirements/wallet without sufficient reward • Cumbersome (price-value of effort) • Irrelevant (infrequent shopper) • Security issues	• Perceived value of rewards • Simplicity of earning • Simplicity of redemption	• Increased lifetime value of shopper (share of wallet, share of require-ments) • Profitability • Involvement/ engagement
Advocacy	• Consumes social capital without sufficient reward • Embarrassing • Cumbersome (price-value of effort) • Security issues	• Enhanced social status - Affiliation or superiority • Perceived value of rewards • Altruism	• Converting new users • Profitability • Creating and enhancing customer relationships • Expanded (virtual) product offering

5

Valuing Advocacy

DON'T LEAVE MONEY ON THE TABLE

The digital world has extended the path to purchase, so that the path leads beyond purchase to advocacy. While attention, participation, and loyalty have financial value, advocacy is probably most important at this point, because it is emerging as a new channel for brand communications.

NET PROMOTER SCORE

In 2006, Fred Reichheld published an article called, "The Microeconomics of Customer Relationships."[1] In it, he described a single metric that correlated with company growth and could be managed concretely, the Net Promoter Score (NPS). The Net Promoter Score is derived from a single question on a customer survey. Responses to the question, "How likely are you to recommend the company to a friend?" are pegged on a 10-point scale, where 1 is "not at all likely" and 10 is "extremely likely." "Promoters" are those customers who answer 9 or 10. "Passives" are those who answer 7 or 8, and "Detractors" are those who respond with a rating of 6 or below. The Net Promoter Score is the percentage of Promoters minus the percentage of Detractors.

This single score was very popular among both general managers and marketing managers for a number of years, and it is not completely out of favor today. There were a few reasons for the popularity of this metric. First, the NPS was touted as an indicator of company growth. Reichheld claimed to find a positive correlation between the NPS and the financial growth of companies across several industries. "Researchers from Bain & Company have found that on average, a 12-point increase in NPS corresponds to a doubling of a company's growth rate, though the variation from one industry to another is substantial."[2] This metric was put forward not as a "nice to know" marketing number, but as a vital marker of company health. Second, the score was easy to understand and calculate. During those years, when the amount of data coming across managers' desks exploded, a single commonsense metric was a welcome piece of sanity. Finally, the elements influencing the response could be addressed in concrete ways. For example, Detractors could be asked in what specific ways they were disappointed with the company or brand. Those issues could become action items for the manager. Many of the reasons for the popularity of the metric are still valid. However, there have been some intervening findings. Two years after Reichheld's article, the same publication released a related article, "Linking Customer Loyalty to Growth."[3] This second article discussed research that had attempted to validate the relationship between the NPS and company growth. Unfortunately, the findings did not validate the NPS. There appeared to be very weak correlation between the NPS and company growth. This report demonstrated that the NPS was not a reliable predictor of future success. The authors drew this conclusion: "Managers who are guided by the

NPS may develop unrealistic views about performance, value and shareholder wealth, leading them to misallocate resources." The authors' methodologies were stringent and their findings convincing. While I would not stake my company's growth on the NPS, I do admire it. The NPS was one of the first attempts to integrate advocacy into the strategic and financial management of a brand. This vision alone is noteworthy. The NPS is also a number that managers can acquire without ruinous cost. Some kinds of advocacy and conversion scores are wonderful, but unrealistically expensive. The simple usefulness of the number was also commendable. The authors of the second article mention this as well. It is worth noting that many executives still find the NPS useful as one general indicator of brand health.

VALUING WORD OF MOUTH

In April 2010, the *McKinsey Quarterly* featured an article on the subject, "A New Way to Measure Word-of-Mouth Marketing."[4] This article made the case for a scientific approach to understanding peer-to-peer brand advocacy. The authors called this "Word-of-Mouth Equity." Their article centered on an equation that was designed to identify the "messages consumers are likely to pass on and the impact of those messages." Here's a shorthand version of the equation: "Volume of Messages × Impact of Those Messages = Word-of-Mouth Equity."

Volume is a scale of magnitude measure. The volume input was fairly straightforward: there could be few messages or many messages. The impact input was more complicated. Impact was expressed as a matrix with four quadrants: Network, Sender, Message Source, and Content. Each of these quadrants had possible positive or negative factors that increased or decreased the impact of the message. For example, in the Network quadrant, impact could be "close and trusted" (positive) or "large and dispersed" (negative). The Content quadrant had "relevant" (positive) or "irrelevant" (negative) messages. The Sender could be influential or noninfluential. Finally, the Source could be based on the sender's personal experience (positive) or on hearsay (negative). The sample equation showed that a few high-impact messages could deliver strong word-of-mouth equity.

This equation provides a mechanism to consider the relevant factors in word-of-mouth marketing. It is a useful tool to help develop strategy in advocacy programming. However, we'll need to go further than this to assess financial value.

When it comes to financial valuation of word-of-mouth programming, there are two standouts, at the time of this writing. The first is a calculation put forward in the *Harvard Business Review* in October 2007.[5]

In this article, the authors calculated both the customer lifetime value (CLV) and the customer referral value (CRV). The CLV is the net present value of a customer's projected contribution (over a set period of time), less the present value of marketing to that person (both acquisition and retention expenditures). This is a fairly straightforward way to evaluate the worth of a customer. Next, CRV was figured this way: the value of customers who joined because of a person's referral (divided by a discount rate) plus the value of customers who would have joined anyway (divided by a discount rate). The authors classified these referrals as Type 1 and Type 2, respectively. By separating the value streams of CLV and CRV for each customer, the authors made an interesting and important discovery. They found that CLV was not predictive of CRV!

This is really different from the assumption that advocates are also the most loyal customers. This assumption seems to creep into the thinking of a number of writers on the subject. For example, Deloitte published an analysis of social media and brand advocacy called, "A New Breed of Brand Advocates." In it, brand advocates were defined through four gates: consumers who have a favorite brand, spend half of their share of requirements (SOR) on that favorite brand, spend more on that brand than the category average, and, finally, engage more often with that brand. The engagement activities included recommending the brand and sharing coupons and information. The consumers who met all of these criteria were called brand advocates. Here the definition of brand advocate included both loyalty (SOR score) and consumption (above-average category consumption). Deloitte conducted a survey among these consumers and drew this conclusion: "Our research found that brand advocates spend two to three times more on their favorite brands, and are on average two to four times more likely to recommend and share."[6] Indeed, it would seem that the brand advocates spent more on average, by Deloitte's initial definition. This study pointed out both how much more the brand advocates were spending and how much more they were advocating relative to average customers, rather than questioning whether these activities were related.

What if consumption is not directly tied to advocacy? Let's go back to the *Harvard Business Review* article and look at a chart of its findings.

LOYALISTS ≠ ADVOCATES

Intriguingly, the chart entitled "The Doing-Saying Gap" indicates that the customers with the highest lifetime values were not those with the highest referral values. Instead, the customers with the highest recruitment rates were solidly in the middle deciles of CLV.

In fact, *none* of the heaviest consumers overlapped with the heaviest advocates. The chart shows 10 tiers of customers, delineated by consumption. The top three advocacy deciles (fifth through seventh) account for more than 70 percent of total referral value, while the top three consumption deciles account for more than 75 percent of total lifetime value. And not one of these deciles overlapped.

Another way to look at this is by customer segment. In this example, the heaviest users had a total customer value (TCV) of $1,973, with 20 percent of this being attributable to referrals. By contrast, the best advocates had a TCV of $1,250, with 82 percent of this being attributable to referrals. Looking at where the customers' contributions are coming from sheds a new light on these groups of users, indicating that their profiles are probably quite different.

These data are based on consumption of a service, not a consumer packaged good (CPG) or other kind of good. So there may be significant variation by category. However, the sheer fact that this *could* occur indicates that it *may* occur elsewhere, just as dramatically and possibly even more dramatically. Imagine luxury goods categories where the halo of social status reflects on advocates, whether they buy or not. Here I am thinking of, say, a consumer using a Tiffany key ring versus wearing a Tiffany engagement ring. In this way, Tiffany caters to both advocates who want a halo effect and big-time buyers. Or conversely, during a recession, a Bergdorf Goodman shopper may stuff her couture into a nameless brown bag, while another shopper buys a designer knockoff from a street vendor.

There are a few big implications. The first is that marketers can't assume that their most loyal customers are their best advocates. This deserves testing on a category-by-category, even brand-by-brand basis. If these are indeed different shopper segments, they should be marketed to differently. I disagree with the authors of the *Harvard Business Review* article that the heavy users should be encouraged to advocate and the advocates to buy more. Instead, I believe it is much easier (and more profitable) to encourage more of the same behaviors than it is to create new ones. Thus, advocates could be given better tools to spread the word and recruit more users and recruiters. Loyalists could be upsold and cross-sold. Furthermore, marketers could construct communications to induce the remainder of their shoppers to fall into one camp or the other (heavy users or heavy advocates). These two audiences should be given different incentives. Incentives for advocacy may differ dramatically from incentives for loyalty.

Finally, of course, marketers need to value these customers' contributions differently. The cost of fueling a customer's advocacy is probably not the same as the cost of retaining a heavily loyal user. All of the deciles in the *Harvard Business Review* chart include both consumption and referral streams, and all customers need to have some marketing that speaks to both activities. However, customers may be segmented by their propensity to advocate or consume, for program development purposes. And they should be valued accordingly.

MAKING IT WORK

Calculating a customer's referral value may be practicable for a business that has detailed information on each customer, such as a telecom company, which is what was used in the *Harvard Business Review* paper. However, for many businesses, calculating referral value for customers has been a challenge. One problem is transaction anonymity. Of course, it is easier to eliminate transaction anonymity online than in-store. Some companies offer to survey a representative sample of online customers to understand the refer-

ral and purchasing dynamic. But today there are even more sophisticated digital tracking tools for online sharing and purchasing.

To date, the best tool out there is Buddy Media's Conversion-
Buddy (see Figure 5.1). ConversionBuddy (http://buddymedia
.com/) provides sharing tools for commercial websites and tracks
all referrals and conversions (and re-referrals!) across major social

| Figure 5.1 | **Advocacy Dashboard** |

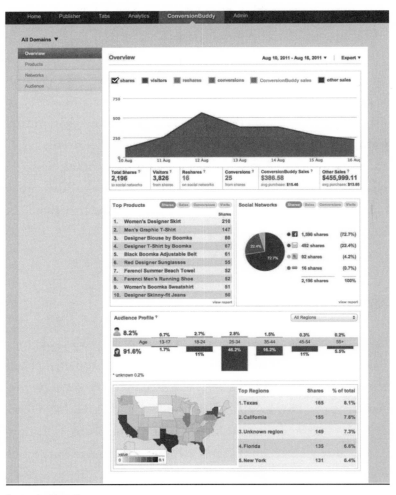

Source: buddymedia.com

platforms. Sales are also tracked by customer and referral, so that real ROI and CRV calculations are possible, and even easy.

Here's how it works. After installing ConversionBuddy's sharing tools on the site, brand managers can use a dashboard to track these metrics: total number of shares, new visits per share, conversion rate, and average revenue per share. Shoppers benefit also. "We credit your customers for the referral, and track the entire process to ensure complete campaign effectiveness and efficiency. Meanwhile, your customers can track their progress toward rewards via a co-branded referral dashboard."[7]

I like this program because of its simplicity for the marketer and the built-in tracking for the advocate who may be earning rewards. In addition to monitoring referrals and sales, ConversionBuddy also tracks the most shared products, the most profitable social platform, and the best advocates, along with their demographics. It takes the guesswork and the labor out of determining advocacy ROI. This is an elegant, practical solution to an urgent business need.

On the other hand, overcoming anonymity at the brick-and-mortar cash wrap can be at least partly addressed with loyalty program incentives, assigning an identifier to each regular buyer. It is in the store itself that a sampling methodology may prove most efficient for those shoppers who are not in the loyalty program. (However, if they are not in the program, they are probably neither heavy advocates nor heavy buyers.)

RATING ADVOCATES

It's possible to talk to, give incentives to, and reward current brand advocates. But what about finding new advocates (beyond those that your customers recruit)? To identify the best advocates, there are several rating services out there, including PeerIndex, Twitter Grader, and Klout, among others. PeerIndex claims to give you "a measure of your online social capital." Twitter Grader pits the communicator against all other tweeters, which produces a score out of 100.

Of these three, Klout seems to be dominating as of this writing. According to their website, "The Klout Score is the measurement of your overall online influence. The scores range from 1 to 100 with higher scores representing a wider and stronger sphere of influence. Klout uses over 35 variables on Facebook and Twitter to measure True Reach, Amplification Probability, and Network Score."[8] Klout's analysis is useful because it also includes a probability that the advocate's audience will "act" (click, look, or participate). This trigger to action is the key for shopper marketers—it's about getting the shopper around the purchase cycle through behavior. Over the last several years, there has been a lot of talk about finding and recruiting influentials (from the book of the same name). Programs like Klout are giving marketers the means to do so.

Getting back to valuing shopper currency, specifically advocacy, it is possible that a brand would offer higher-value incentives to those with higher Klout scores. In other words, shoppers may begin to financially leverage their social capital. This is an era in which shoppers can begin to use their social rating, instead of their credit rating, to earn currency. The shopper is the marketer's new media vehicle—and those with higher ratings will want higher fees.

ADVOCATING BY CATEGORY

There is some evidence that consumers don't advocate for all categories equally. Some categories are more likely to be recommended and reviewed than others. Conversely, not all shoppers rely on reviews or recommendations equally.

Studies show that consumers advocate heavily in some categories and significantly less so in others. The implication is that certain categories will be able to rely on advocacy to a much greater extent than others. This knowledge will affect the marketing budget, spending priorities, and strategy. So, the first order of business in planning strategy and developing financial targets is understanding where one's category falls in the spectrum of social influence.

FOR LOVE OR MONEY

So far, we have been talking about "paid" advocates. The Holy Grail is to recruit a group of consumers who are so aligned with the brand that they advocate for free. I call these people *brand evangels*. Their motive is much deeper than material compensation. They are moved by the values and mission of the brand.

Simon Sinek, author of *Start with Why* (http://www.startwithwhy.com/), draws a sharp line between brand loyalists and repeat business. Repeat business can be manipulated through promotions, incentives, and other such means. Real loyalty, on the other hand, is deeper. According to Sinek, "Repeat business is when people do business with you multiple times. Loyalty is when people are willing to turn down a better product or a better price to continue doing business with you. Loyal customers often don't even bother to research the competition or entertain other options. Loyalty is not easily won. Repeat business, however, is."[9]

Sinek's contention is that genuine leaders, including brand leaders, always know why they are doing what they are doing. Their "why" is the reason they get up in the morning; how and what they do simply follow as a result. Leaders embody their values in every action. Using this approach, it is easy to understand why people tattoo brands on their arms (Harley-Davidson, Hello Kitty, and so on). By showing the brand, people are showing their personal values.

Let's go back to an example from Chapter 2, lululemon athletica. This brand makes women's (and men's) athletic gear, especially yoga pants, aerobic outfits, and running gear. Its philosophy is embodied in its manifesto, which is found online and in-store and is printed on the side of every shopping bag. Lululemon's affirmations are optimistic and plucky, including slogans like these: "Dance, Sing, Floss, and Travel" and "Listen, Listen, Listen and then Ask Strategic Questions."

How does lululemon handle brand advocacy? It lets brand shoppers apply to be "lululemon ambassadors." The application

Social Vending Machines

In April 2011, news broke that Pepsi was introducing the first "social vending machine." This machine allows users to buy a Pepsi for a friend using their mobile number. "Pepsi's new system lets users give their friends a beverage gift by entering the recipient's name, mobile phone number, and a personalized text message or video. The gift is delivered with a system code and instructions to redeem it at any similar machine." [10]

While this prototype machine didn't have a social media (Facebook-type) interface, the news is still significant from a shopper currency standpoint. If shoppers can influence friends at the point of sale digitally at checkout, there may be a huge opportunity for future advocacy programming. Imagine a similar interface at a retail store with self-checkout, such as a grocery store or kiosk. This kind of thing (as through tweeting or gifting) is already available at self-checkout for many virtual stores.

includes an area for an essay on how the brand manifesto speaks to the applicant. There are two levels of ambassadors: community level and elite. The elite level includes Olympic athletes. Here is an excerpt from the company's website about the program.

> The lululemon ambassador program is extended to unique individuals in our store communities who embody the lululemon lifestyle and live our culture.
>
> Our elite ambassadors are our international rock stars, athletes of an elite level (think Olympians) that choose to train and/or compete in our fantastic product because it is the best in the world. Further to that, they are members of our lululemon family. We don't pay athletes to wear our clothes, as that's just not the way we roll. Instead, we support them with product and anything else (within reason) they request from us— e.g., yoga classes, training accommodation and our personal favourite, the LEAFs (lululemon elite ambassador fan club).[11]

I remember when lululemon opened a store in my hometown. Since I am a person who frequents several gyms and dance studios around town, I got plenty of exposure to the brand and its advocates. Amazingly, the brand advocates (evangels) are every bit as upbeat and high-minded as their brand. Clearly this brand has values that are being embraced by its shopper base.

CASE STUDIES

Pretzel Crisps

Many advocacy programs are managed from Facebook. A new product, Pretzel Crisps, launched its page on Facebook and wanted to gain fans and buzz. To get a quick following, the brand rewarded surfers with a coupon for "liking" the brand. This is simple compensation for an endorsement. Here is a recap of the case, sourced through eMarketer and Buddy Media.

Goal: Pretzel Crisps wanted to create a fan base on Facebook and induce trial by word of mouth.

Program: On February 24, 2011, Pretzel Crisps unveiled a Facebook exclusive coupon for fans only. This custom coupon, hidden behind a "fan-gate," encouraged users to become fans and print a coupon at home. Pretzel Crisps also offered this news to its network of bloggers and enabled friendly blogs to exclusively promote the offer, further establishing the brand's relationship with its advocates and champions. By staggering the news of the coupon, Pretzel Crisps managed to maximize the impact of this "mini-campaign."

Interim Results: Fans increased from 6,800 to 13,700 in a two-week period. Coupon redemption soared to 87 percent.

The brand changed the coupon offer to a buy-one-get-one (BOGO), available for only two weeks. There was no corporate announcement about the change.

Results: Fans doubled to 29,000 in two days, and the redemption on the BOGO was 95 percent. "According to IRI data, Pretzel Crisp sales grew 93% for the 52-week period ending July 10, 2011, vs. the same period the previous year. For the 12-week period ending July 10, the brand experienced 131% growth."[12]

There have been discussions in the press about "buying likers," and several bloggers have cautioned businesses about the dangers of this practice.[13] But most of these writers are not denouncing promotions; instead, they are condemning the practice of buying blogging shills, who are paid to "like" a product on social media. Most of these shills are enlisted by middlemen, who are, in turn, selling those lists to brands. From a revenue perspective, these fans don't translate into sales. On the other hand, legitimate fans, legitimate bloggers, and authentic likers often do convert to buyers. Buddy Media claims an average 10.9 percent conversion rate for Facebook "shares" that lead to purchases.

Advocacy is sometimes used not only to improve short-term revenue, but also to gain brand awareness and attention through social buzz. Brand imagery can be communicated with buzz and engagement, and potential buyers can get an idea of brand cohorts. Advocacy works as engagement, buzz, and cohort affiliation, especially for higher-ticket items like luxury brands and travel.

Carnival Cruises

People love to share their vacation memories and photos; Carnival Cruises gives them the chance to do so with the "didja ever?" tab. This tab highlights pictures of cruisers doing something for the first time, such as catching a fish, snorkeling, or holding an exotic bird. The brand also features a "send a message" link (with a menu of messages and photos) to quickly post a vacation sentiment on one's personal wall. Alternatively, a cruiser can give one of six Carnival Cruise digital "gifts" to online friends.

> *Goal: The company was an early adopter of social media and wanted to tap into the power of Facebook and other social channels to accelerate its growth, create an online fan base, and track sales from earned media.*
>
> *Program: Carnival Cruises sought to use social media to replicate the cruise experience online and extend the experience, both before and after travel. Specifically, on the "Carnival Magic" Facebook page tab, fans could view videos, interact with Carnival*

crew members, and post feedback, all while sharing these experiences with friends.

Results: At the end of 2009, when Carnival Cruise Lines launched its Facebook presence, the company had about 45,000 Facebook fans or "likes." Now Carnival is up to about 335,000 "likes."

"In general, Facebook has been a big success for us," said Stephanie Leavitt, senior manager, online engagement at Carnival Cruise Lines. "We have really qualified traffic coming from Facebook and going back to Carnival.com. Our Facebook branded tab performs the best . . . we have seen sales as a side effect. It's not really our objective, but we do track it so we can see if somebody came back and actually booked a cruise."[14]

While this program is working well relative to the objectives of buzz and brand experience, there are also opportunities to use branded currency to reward behaviors. Carnival Cruises have "onboard credits" that are redeemable at sea for things like drinks and extras. In fact, the brand gives shoppers incentives to book their trips early by offering discounts along with "onboard credits." These credits would work well in giving incentives for advocacy—getting friends and family to book cruises too. This currency could also drive loyalty or "next purchases" by rewarding sharing after the cruise. Facebook has announced that it has bought Push Pop Press, which will give consumers more sophisticated ways to share their stories on Facebook. Improvements in technology such as this will only enhance programs like Carnival Cruise's.

In order to get an insider's view of advocating online, I spoke with Michael Lazerow, CEO of Buddy Media and longtime Internet entrepreneur.

INTERVIEW WITH MICHAEL LAZEROW, CEO, BUDDY MEDIA

Michael is a serial entrepreneur who has cofounded four successful Internet-based media companies. He has a passion for creating, managing, and growing companies from the ground up. Michael is currently chairman and CEO of Buddy Media, Inc., a New York–based company whose Facebook management system, the Buddy Media Platform, is used by eight out of the top ten global advertisers.

Q: What makes advocacy an enticing business proposition?

A: *We're in a world where the difference between a good company and a great company is how much your customers are willing to talk about you. Building those connections is the key to driving a brand's business. But positive word of mouth isn't only digital; face-to-face advocacy is not dead.*

Q: Typically, how would a client evaluate an advocacy program?

A: *There are two ways to evaluate advocacy. First, there are referrals and sales. By referrals, I mean more than just "liking" the brand. Referral measures include how many shares, tweets, retweets, embeds, and people proactively referring the brand there are. Then, there are the sales that result from that.*

    Second, an increase in conversation volume is highly correlated with business results. If people are talking about your product (and here I don't mean about a negative issue, like a product recall), then sales, share of market, and stock prices all trend upward. Let's take mobile phones. At the top, you have Apple and Android getting a lot of conversation. Next there is Nokia. If you map its units and ship-

ments against the level of conversation, you can see a high correlation. Using this measure, you could have seen that Nokia was in trouble even before it lost share.

I still like the net promoter score as a qualitative, directional data point. I would never say, "Let's hang our hat on this." However, rolled into a macro view with year-over-year numbers and other data points, it works.

The power of ConversionBuddy is that we can actually see how links and content are shared and reshared, and specifically how they drive conversions, whether those conversions be sales, product demo sign-ups, contest entries, or something else. All of the embeds, the URL shortening, and the analytics are bundled into one elegant solution.

Q: What do you think advocacy and sharing will look like in the future?

A: *At the end of the day, it's the technology that's changing, not people. People still like to share water-cooler information: Where do you like to go for dinner? Who is a good hairdresser? That's what we talk about. The speed and the friction are the elements that will change with technology. The speed increases and the friction decreases.*

We've gone from a world in which standards change every five years to one in which standards change every few months. The rate of change is accelerating for everyone—shoppers and businesses alike.

In the future, you will have easy access to the right information, at the right time, in the right place as you make decisions or seek information. You will know which movie to see or which pair of pants to buy, using your social graph or your extended interest graph. The future will have a frictionless, always-on social graph wherever you go. We'll also see better crowdsourcing technology for causes and other issues.

Of course net neutrality is very important. Does the stuff to consumers get through to whom it's intended for? This is an important part of the discussion in Washington. Of course, I am on the side of net neutrality and more freedom.

Also, bandwidth may become cheaper as technology gets better at compression. This means that there will be smarter ways to send and store information. Digital payments will get easier and cheaper, too.

Q: What are the most important issues *today* with advocacy and sharing programs?

A: *One of the most important issues today is how we are evaluating advocacy. We know that your most profitable customers aren't necessarily the ones who buy the most stuff from you. For example, if you have customer levels, tiered by who spends the most, often the lower-tiered customers are responsible for more profit. The reason is that they could be advocating your brand more aggressively.*

> *The average Facebook share generates $2.10 in incremental sales.*
>
> *The average conversion rate for a Facebook share was 10.2 percent.*
>
> *The most sharing for Internet retailers occurs on Wednesdays and Thursdays.*
>
> *The "magic hour" for Internet retailers is 12:13 p.m.–1:45 p.m. on weekdays.*
>
> *On Facebook, 27–33-year-old women are the most active sharers and drive the highest conversion rates.*
>
> *Twitter drives the highest click-through rate but has much lower conversion rates than Facebook and e-mail sharing.[15]*

The higher the price point of the brand, the tighter the social graph. It's like airplane owners or yacht people; these are very tight social graphs and very high price points. There are always tighter graphs around high-passion and high-price-point items. It's different from categories like soft drinks and beer.

Q: Could you comment on advocates?

A: *The advocates are the people who care more about reputation and community. They share because they're trusted for sharing. They have earned status in their community. For the advocates, it's not about the power of their money, it's about the power of their social capital.*

There are some implications for marketing to advocates in the digital realm. At Buddy Media, we track which products are most shared and least shared, among many other metrics. One interesting example is that if you look at the Victoria's Secret Diamond Bra, which has come out every year since 2001, it's shared like crazy! Yet, how many people actually buy that? But those shares, the conversation, lead to the sales of other Victoria's Secret products.

An immediate implication for brands is reprogramming the splash page based on what is likely to be shared. Today the top-selling product isn't on the home page—instead, it's the top-shared product. That is why the New York Times *has "the most e-mailed" list on its home page. Do you remember the woman who took a month to train killer whales and then wrote a book on training husbands? The editors would have never elected to put that on the landing page. Yet, this story and book review went out to tens of thousands.*

CHAPTER 5 Recap: *Valuing Advocacy*

Using a word-of-mouth equity equation is a useful way to think about developing strategy for an advocacy program. "Volume of Messages × Impact of Those Messages = Word-of-Mouth Equity." (McKinsey Quarterly, April 2010)

- Marketers can't assume that their most loyal customers are their best advocates. These may be two very different groups of users. This deserves testing on a category-by-category, even brand-by-brand, basis. If loyalists are a different group from advocates:
  - Don't market to them or give them incentives the same way.
  - Don't value them the same way financially.

- Consider using the *Harvard Business Review*'s formulas for customer lifetime value (CLV) and customer referral value (CRV) as a starting point for strategy.
  - The CLV is the net present value of a customer's projected contribution (over a set period of time) less the present value of marketing to that person (both acquisition and retention expenditures). This is a fairly straightforward way to evaluate the financial worth of a customer.
  - The CRV is the value of customers who joined because of a person's referral (divided by a discount rate) plus the value of customers who would have joined anyway (divided by a discount rate).

- To track real-time brand referrals, re-referrals, and resulting sales by product and by social platform, consider using real-time census tracking data for online business. There may be more of these kinds of tracking services coming, but Buddy Media has it figured out now.

- Brands may begin to offer higher-value incentives to those with higher Klout scores, in exchange for advocacy behaviors. In other words, shoppers may begin to financially leverage their social capital in the context of the shopper economy.
- "Brand evangels" are consumers who are so aligned with the brand that they advocate for free. This is the Holy Grail of marketing. Evangels indicate a strong brand and profitability too. However, it may not be realistic to think that every brand will have only brand evangels and no advocates who have been given incentives.

6

Advocates and Evangels

INFLUENCING THE INFLUENCERS

No discussion of advocacy or evangelism would be complete without a few words from the advocates and brand fans themselves. I wanted to hear the reasons advocates do what they do, from their own mouths and keyboards. Toward this end, I talked to and researched three types of advocates: influencers (bloggers), ordinary Netizen advocates, and brand evangels.

To understand the blogging community, I asked Collective Bias (CB) to help me. CB has an established blogger community called Social Fabric with a proven track record of engagement.

Here's how CB describes itself: "Collective Bias, a shopper media agency, builds true relationships between brands, retailers and consumers through its proprietary social influencer platform called Social Fabric. The Social Fabric community drives conversations on a wide variety of social media platforms in order to build consumer engagement and brand loyalty that lead to sales conversion."[1]

Collective Bias and I fielded a survey to 30 bloggers in the Social Fabric™ community in the spring of 2011. While some of the questions were binary (yes/no), most were open-ended, allowing bloggers to explain why or how they approached an advocacy task. Here are the findings of this qualitative study.

Collective Bias—The Bloggers' Perspective

The questions in the survey dealt with motivations for recommendations, ratings, and reviews and how the bloggers felt about incentives.

The first question asked, "Have you ever recommended a product to your readers that you did not like?" More than 80 percent of the respondents claimed to have never recommended a product that they personally didn't like. However, among the 20 percent who had done so, the reason was the same. These advocates did so because, "I thought my readers may like it, even though I did not."

Nearly two-thirds of respondents agreed that it is acceptable for brands to provide incentives to bloggers and advocates who rate, review, or "like" products. While this may seem like a high percentage, virtually everyone in this group gave his response with a certain proviso about editorial independence, such as, "If it is a product that I already am going to endorse, I have no problem with this method. However, I will not have my own opinion 'bought.'" Advocates felt that the incentives, whether free product, money, sponsorships, or discounts, weren't influencing their reviews or opinions. In fact, a substantial portion of the compensated bloggers felt that they deserved to get something for the time and effort of reviewing a product. They viewed this as a kind of payment for the labor of product testing and writing, rather than an incentive for a positive review. Said one blogger, "There's nothing wrong with being compensated for your time as a reviewer."

A smaller percentage of bloggers was undecided about the matter. However, practically speaking, it seems that their point of view was quite similar to that of those who claimed that it was okay. This comment is typical of respondents who were undecided: "This is somewhat of a gray area for me. I am sometimes compensated for my honest reviews—does that count as an 'incentive' for reviewing? If so, then I agree that it is all right, as long as I am not told what to say and can be completely honest." Those who felt that *any* compensation compromised the review were in the single digits.

In fact, all but three of the bloggers claimed to have taken some sort of compensation for a review, rating, or recommendation. The most frequent compensation cited was free product, followed by sponsorship, monetary incentives, and, rarely, coupons. A few claimed never to have taken any incentive for ratings or reviews.

Most of those who accepted free product or even monetary rewards were very clear in stating that they considered this to be compensation for their time or for the review itself, rather than for a positive review per se.

When asked how they determined when it was okay to take an incentive, there were several consistent answers. The first had to do with disclosure. Transparency makes the incentive acceptable—full disclosure is the policy of most bloggers on CB. According to one respondent, "As long as I have a full disclosure on every post, I am okay with accepting product and payment. My opinions are my own, whether I was compensated or not!" However, it is unclear whether this holds true outside of the Social Fabric community.

Accepting compensation is also tolerable if there is a lack of pressure about the content of the review. One blogger stated, "I will take an incentive as long as I have control over the content being published. I will not just republish a press release." Another blogger said, "I will take an incentive only if I am given freedom to write a completely honest review of my experience." Interestingly, one advocate gives the choice about running a negative review to the company. She said, "I will review a product if I think I will like it. If I am wrong (and I don't like it), I offer to not run the review—that is, to say nothing rather than say something negative. I let the company decide if it wants me to run it. I don't think paid reviews exist; that is advertising, which is fine, but call it what it is."

In terms of writing positive reviews, the group cited several reasons for them. First, the bloggers said that they are motivated to write positive reviews about brands that provide high quality with good customer service. They want to write something positive about brands that they like, or that their family likes. They are also motivated by specific causes, such as education or the environment. Sometimes a brand's values will align with the advocate's, making the recommendation a sincere endorsement. "If I personally like the product and brand, I will always recommend it. A lot of times I'll talk about a product I love and never have been offered an incentive in any way. I just like to talk about products I am passionate about."

Interestingly, only one person claimed that products that aligned with the blog content were motivating. Others asserted that they would recommend products that "fit the lifestyle" of their readers, but the editorial context of the blog itself was cited only once.

The reasons for writing a negative review were very consistent across respondents. Poor product quality and dubious corporate ethics were most frequently cited as the prompts for a poor review. The comments on deficient product quality ranged from "anything cheaply made or full of artificial ingredients" to product performance, "if it doesn't do what it says it will do." Advocates dinged companies with dodgy ethics; they stated that they would give a negative review "when the company blatantly lies or tries to hide factors about a product" or "if the company is not responsive."

Many bloggers would avoid writing a review altogether, or would give a low rating, if they simply didn't like or have a use for the product personally. For example, one person said that she wouldn't write a recommendation "if it doesn't fit my lifestyle. For example, I do not have babies, so I would not recommend baby products unless it was something I used when my children were young."

Interestingly, while courtesy to the blogger was cited only once as an impetus for a positive review, a lack of respect was frequently cited as a reason for a poor review. Poor professionalism seems to have a halo effect on the company and its products. Here is one reviewer's perspective: "[I am motivated to *not* recommend a brand] when the PR person, or people working for them, are rude, pushy, or don't bother to know me (generic forms sent with wrong names or blog name in it). Or when they ask me to spread the good word about their product, even if I have never tried it. Sorry, not happening."

Finally, we were curious about whether the bloggers doubted the authenticity of other recommendations that they read on the web. The answer was a resounding yes. The blogging community in particular knows which companies are sending out press releases and samples. When a blogger simply cuts and pastes copy from the press release, this sends a red flag to others who are in the know. "Of course I get the same pitches everyone else does, and when I read a post that is just a cut and paste of a press release, I doubt it." Another reviewer complained, "Often it seems like blogs are just reposting press releases. That makes all of us look bad!"

Curiously, it was the compensation itself that seems to cast a shadow on the credibility of the other bloggers, in the minds of those interviewed. This was counterintuitive because the majority of bloggers claimed that they didn't mind taking compensation, especially if their review would have been positive anyway. In other words, if the reviewer likes the product, taking an incentive creates no dissonance. However, even when another blogger discloses his compensation, the review is called into question.

- "If I read a recommendation that is all rosy and over the top and then find out the writer received compensation, I am a little leery about the honesty of the review."

- "I read a lot of blogs, and I question the authenticity of a recommendation all the time. Even with myself. It's hard to believe a person is being honest when you discover there was an incentive. You have to use your own filter and base your judgments on a person's work in other networks or on their blog."

- "I question the authenticity if it was a celebrity endorsement, because half the time I don't believe they use the brand for any other reason than to get paid."

Looking at these responses confused me. Bloggers said that they felt comfortable taking compensation for writing a review, especially if they liked the product anyway and disclosed the compensation to their readers. So, how could these same people *doubt the sincerity* of another reviewer in the same position?

In order to make sense of this seeming contradiction, I consulted psychologist Dr. Jeff Johnson, former EVP and general manager of Cramer-Krasselt, a New York–based ad agency, and author of the book *The Hourglass Solution: A Boomer's Guide to the Rest of Your Life*. His response was:

The world of blogging has grown up without either the legal or industry self-imposed ethical standards that exist in advertising, public relations, and journalism. The separation between editorial and advertising, for example, has been (at least historically) keenly observed by most professional publications.

Bloggers, however, find themselves operating across both sides of the aisle—they write the editorial content and they collect the marketing revenue. So the temptation to capitalize on this is surely foremost in a blogger's mind, even if they do not act upon it. Given the prominence of such temptation, it's not surprising that most bloggers believe that "others" are likely to succumb.

I've not seen any psychological research on bloggers accepting corporate money, but relevant psychological studies have shown that when research participants are paid to rate a product, they become even more strongly convinced that their rating was objective than participants who were not paid. People want to believe that they are honest—and the more external evidence to the contrary, the more internal evidence they muster up.

And this is precisely why they believe that other bloggers behave unethically when faced with a similar situation (i.e., being paid to rate a product). All bloggers know that "some bloggers" are unethical. The more they point fingers at other bloggers, the better their own behavior feels.

ADVOCACY ROUNDTABLE

John Andrews, CEO and cofounder, Collective Bias
Amy Callahan, cofounder and chief of staff
Ted Rubin, chief social marketing officer

There is an old adage that goes something like this: a satisfied customer tells 3 friends and a dissatisfied one tells 10. Yet, according to market research firm Keller Fay Group, "87% of consumers tend to write reviews when they have positive things to say."[2]

Q: Based on your experience in the world of social networking, do you think that's true?

JOHN: *When people are passionate and they express themselves, it's a way to feel connected to a brand. When I was at Walmart, our early reviews and ratings were some of the first social media. For the first time, shoppers could talk back. We found that the average rating was 3.5 or 3.6 out of 5. That is statistically better than the median.*

Possibly the most valuable word-of-mouth impact is from the pissed-off guy whose problem was fixed. Now he's a convert. He's telling 100 people about his experience. It's like the consumer has a megaphone at his disposal and can tell the world.

TED: *I agree with the research that most reviews are positive. In fact, 40 to 60 percent of consumers will advocate if they are given the tools to do so. In my opinion, all of these companies are nervous about how they may be reviewed, but they should understand that much more good is said than bad.*

AMY: *I agree with Ted. Consumers have a public voice now. They are asking for help or want the company to hear them. It may seem that negative feedback is increasing, but that's because we are hearing from them more.*

TED: *Negative feedback has always existed. For the most part, consumers want to be heard and recognized. They are not always looking for resolution.*

For example, JetBlue does a great job of this. In 99 percent of the cases, its employees can't solve your problem, because the delay or problem is beyond their control. But they can speak to you, let you share, and give you information about when the problem may be resolved and what's going on. As a customer, I feel great because I feel impor-

tant, informed, and in control. Sometimes JetBlue will offer a thousand free miles on a delayed flight. That feels good too.

People love to share good stuff. Think about a friend that is always bitching. Enough already! After a while, you tune out. But if you hear a good thing, you keep listening. People love to hear about a good experience or, say, a good movie or restaurant.

Brands need to give consumers easy options to share. I like to put things in my own words, but if the company has a preset message and I am happy with the company, I'll just hit the send button. The option to edit the share keeps it real.

In the survey, several bloggers complained about poor professionalism on the part of the companies that reach out to them for reviews. Lack of respect and responsiveness seemed to create a halo of negativity around the company and its products for the bloggers.

Q: What specific actions can companies take to show positive regard for the blogging community and potential reviewers across social media?

JOHN: *Companies need to simply take the time and energy to learn something about the people they are reaching out to. It's not heavy lifting. It's reading some of the blogger's content and making a few comments. The bloggers say that those comments are solid gold. It's an investment of the reader's time and energy to write something.*

TED: *Companies don't understand the blogger community. To them, it's another media buy. Mostly agencies are reaching out on behalf of the brands. This creates two problems. First, they regard the bloggers like another AOL or business property. And they treat them the same way.*

Because the blogger is another salesperson in their eyes, they will blow off interviews. This alienates the bloggers. Most of the bloggers have jobs, children, and many other responsibilities. In order to do an interview, a blogger needs to arrange for child care or walk out of the office to get privacy. The way that agencies work, they aren't built to foster relationships because everything needs to be billed to a client. If that time can't be billed to a client, it falls to the bottom of the to-do list. They aren't built for this business model.

For example, let's say a toy company wants to set up 50 bloggers to write about a new product. Well, agencies will send a beauty blogger a request for a toy review.

AMY: *Also, the requests are anonymous. "Dear INSERT BLOGGER NAME HERE:" The agency didn't even enter the name. One simple fix is to personalize it. Name them.*

TED: *The checks are paid on business terms, like net 60. Well, she needs that money for Christmas, so that doesn't work. They treat her like she's a big company.*

Let's say a blogger wants to do more business with the toy company, but the company doesn't have time to deal with the bloggers or build a relationship. She calls and they ignore her.

Now the bloggers will mention you any chance they get, if they like you. If you ignore them, that won't happen. The fix here is to assign someone to handle the blogger community, to get to know them and to treat them fairly.

TED: *I remember a while back a cosmetic executive at a Fortune 100 company made an inappropriate presentation to bloggers. It was a marketing presentation, which should have been delivered to his management team. He was bragging about how he leveraged bloggers' efforts financially. This didn't go over very well with the bloggers.*

At the end of the day, you pay them for their influence. Bloggers work long and hard to get people to pay attention, and they should be compensated. We aren't paying for advocacy, but for influence. Critics are valuable and do add some authenticity . . . if 100 percent of the comments are positive, it isn't realistic.

Q: One of the blogger respondents claimed that even when a book is panned, the sales go up. Can you explain this?

JOHN: *If everything is unicorns and kittens, it is not believable. A pan from a blogger is as interesting to me as a positive review. Let's face it, there are differences of opinion; a customer's not liking the product doesn't have to be bad. Passionate and heartfelt is good. Even slamming is okay. If you read 20 of them, then you have a problem.*

TED: *It's the old adage that any news is good news. In the early days of my career, I worked in the investment banking community. Our company's CEO was on the cover of* Forbes *at the center of a very negative article. And he made reprints for everyone!*

In today's environment, you can't control the negative comments. But that's okay, because there's the curiosity factor—everyone wants to see what the buzz is about!

Q: What are the most important issues for companies that are trying to recruit brand advocates?

JOHN: *What people want to talk about and what the company wants to talk about are often not the same. Marrying the brand message to what's engaging to consumers is a different skill from the old-school communication methods, which are push-type communications.*

For example, when a customer posts a negative review and there are crickets, no one at the company is responding. It's a giveaway that the company isn't really interested in engaging its consumers. It's a push PR effort. But these are the real places to start in advocacy, because these are hand-raisers. It is worthwhile to find out what's compelling about the brand to those folks.

Companies also need to be open to whoever is responding to the brand. I have seen a number of company-driven consumer profiles, where a client was convinced that its target was characterized by x and y. But in the real world, we saw that people who liked the product fit a different profile. Their profile was different from the one that was sanctioned, and the shopper was dismissed. Be open.

Another typical thing brands do is find the "top 10 bloggers." But the top 10 bloggers today are media properties. The top 10 may not be discussing the relevant product category at all. These blogger properties are monetizing their streams at the highest level, and they won't be happy with free product.

The solution is that companies need to go deep into the community. The most relevant bloggers for the category may not be the highest-reach people, but they are the 20 to 30 people really writing about the category and the brands.

The blogger space is developing into a channel like other channels. The questions are, "Who is supporting my brand? Whom should I support?"

AMY: *Bloggers get an average of 25 to 30 pitches a week. Mostly these occur on Monday through Wednesday. Pitches and new product launches can easily get lost, but you will get attention if you have taken the time to build a relationship.*

TED: *Yes, competition and getting yourself to the top of the heap—those are the issues.*

Companies need to dedicate someone to reaching out to the blog-gers. It is important for that person to stay in front of them.

For example, I give out my personal phone number and e-mail on Twitter. The brands can do this too. Both bloggers and regular con-sumers feel good if you are accessible. I know I can give my number out because very few people ever call me. They just want to know I'm there.

I can't tell you how many people have approached me at confer-ences to thank me for being available and to ask how I do it. I can do it because I know that not many actually take advantage of the acces-sibility . . . but I am available if they do.

We've been talking about bloggers, of course, but they are only one small part of the brand advocates. Most companies spend a huge amount of money to acquire new customers versus retaining the old customers. They could give a "promotion" to their advocates for a lot less money and get a bigger bang for their buck.

AMY: *It's true. Companies and agencies are out there looking for the biggest bloggers; instead, they should be finding those people who already like the brand.*

Q: What about rating services like Klout?

JOHN: *I am very intrigued by these rating systems. We were experi-menting with these the other day and came up with a "KLOUT CAGE MATCH." It's a little program where you put in two brands and they have a Klout fight.*

Brands are looking for something to hang their hat on; they want a measurement tool, so Klout is filling that role. The question is, how does the algorithm stack up versus the brand's goals?

TED: *These tools are coming to be used all the time now, and we need to get used to them. Klout has done a great job of selling itself.*

Corporate America likes it. This means watching your score and figuring out how the score is developed. Klout is even being used in the context of job interviews.

Q: What are the most important issues for consumers who are reviewing products?

JOHN: *Transparency. It's not wrong or unethical to have a monetary relationship, but this should be disclosed.*

Another issue for reviewers is what happens with the feedback. Walmart used the feedback from the original 12 mommy bloggers for new product development. This showed the bloggers their real worth and validated their efforts.

TED: *Some bloggers don't think any money should change hands at all. Others have no problem with this. Clarification about when it's okay and when it's not would benefit everyone in the community.*

Q: Where do you see advocacy heading in the next five years?

JOHN: *Everyone today is both a content creator and a content consumer. There will be ways to aggregate that consumer-created content into media to help shoppers. For example, toothpaste reviews—Google is aggregating the 40 reviews on walmart.com and the dozen on CVS .com into one stream about toothpaste. We will choose our streams of media along the shopping path. In this case, I would rather know what my friend Liz thinks about the toothpaste than what some guru thinks about it. Getting that information organically and seamlessly is part of the process of influencing that person as he enters into shopper mode. Most people aren't going onto Facebook to shop right now. So in the next five years, companies will need to figure out how to turn those consumer-created streams of media into properties, as we know them today.*

TED: *Technology and social media will become more entrenched in the world around us and in appliances and objects. The change will be how things are linked with other things, like between your car and a retailer, for example. Sears is working hard to make this happen. Appliances will be linked too. Refrigerators will be putting items on the shopping list.*

We will also see more of the Google Plus–type segmentation in social media. This will make it harder to keep up with, but more like the real world. You will have circles of friends. You have only certain conversations with business colleagues, your family, and the bowling team.

Up until now, people have used social media as a broadcast medium, not to build relationships. Going forward, we will be forced to segment.

AMY: *We've only scratched the surface.*

TED: *I made a joke a few days ago that my head is like a Twitter feed, with thoughts and ideas constantly scrolling through. In the future, maybe we will be able to think of a tweet and it will be sent to followers. There is technology that makes this possible in some mechanical realms.*

NETIZEN BRAND ADVOCATES ("REGULAR," NONBLOGGING USERS OF THE INTERNET)

We've talked to highly influential people on the web about their attitudes toward brand advocacy. Next, let's take a look at the reasons that ordinary citizens of the Net (Netizens) have for advocating.

First, regular Net surfing shoppers are given incentives to advocate in exchange for value, like virtual currency, coupons, or free stuff. If they are rewarded directly, they may advocate, which can include anything from "liking" a brand on Facebook to writing a review. For example, in August of 2011, Dunkin' Donuts offered virtual goods to fans who "liked" the brand on Facebook. "*LAST CHANCE! It's your last chance to claim your free gifts for liking The Sims Social. They expire very soon so claim now before they go!*"[3] To some extent, this approach trains consumers to expect rewards for their efforts. Look at these quotes scraped from the Dunkin' Donuts Facebook Fan Page.[4]

- "If we like you, we should be rewarded! We are advertising for you. HINT!"

- "I thought I would get a free sample of the K cup by "liking." I liked, and I see no info on how to get my coffee! What's up?"

Clearly, personal rewards for advocating are appreciated, even if the consumer is already a brand fan. For example, American Express cardholders are rewarded with 5,000 bonus points for each approved referral. This is a heck of an incentive. Even so, I am not convinced that this sours the relationship. It's like giving a gift to a friend. Sometimes for a birthday or even for no particular occasion, a friend will pick up the dinner tab. It's a gesture of goodwill and friendliness. However, when these rewards come from a brand, consumers may begin to expect them as a matter of course, effectively creating another cost of doing business. Indeed, these rewards may become a cost of doing business regardless of how brands feel about them.

Another reason that nonblogging consumers pass along brand messages, or endorse brands socially, is to benefit the recipient. *Benefit* is a pretty broad word here. Benefits to others can include anything from education and information to entertainment to coupons, deals, and outright gifts. The motive is to benefit the giftee, but branding and advocacy are still taking place. An example of this was the Bud Light page on Facebook in 2009. It allowed users "to send friends gifts carrying the Bud Light logo. When you send a friend a virtual Bud Light, the gift will appear on his or her wall with any message you choose to include. This will then be seen in the updates on all of his or her friends' home pages, potentially putting the brand in front of a large group of people every time a gift is sent."[5] The Bud Light virtual gift is friendly and fun, but it is clearly also advocacy and branded messaging.

Most brand rewards are structured to benefit both the giver and the receiver. For example, a company called SocialTwist offers brands a "Tell-A-Friend" program. A case on the SocialTwist website shows that Jimmy Dean sausages offered a $1 coupon to shoppers, but increased the coupon to $2.50 if the shopper shared the offer with three or more friends.[6] This kind of everybody-wins programming is quickly becoming the standard.

In another example, World of Warcraft (WoW) offered the opportunity for advocates to "level up" quickly (advance levels in the game), and even give away levels to a friend, if the referred friend bought time in the game. According to one user comment, "If you play the game and have an 80 and your friend wants to play with you, it's not fun to level again with them in general. . . . This way when leveling together u have 3x xp [triple experience points] to get them closer to you. That's the rationale." This refer-a-friend program benefits both players by enabling them to play together in a more satisfying way. However, while this program did recruit players, some of them were "gaming" the system. Gaming rewards programs is nothing new, but it deserves to be mentioned. Here are one player's remarks about the WoW recruitment program: "So this means you could recruit yourself 3 times, build a shaman chain, and level them together with triple XP [experience points] then get a 4 character to level 60 in min's. And Blizzard don't think this may attract some power-leveling services to abuse the system? Making it easier to level will only create more cowboy services offering ever cheaper levelling services. I for one don't think this is a good idea."[7]

This kind of double-dealing is similar to couponers who copy coupons to get more discounting than the original program intended. Gaming the system will always be with us, and as usual, smart marketers need to be mindful of it when constructing any value exchange.

THE EVANGELS' PERSPECTIVE

Evangels are different from advocates in that they are promoting a brand without anticipating any compensation. Recompense may come, but the primary motive for an evangel is to spread the good word about the brand. Evangels are self-proclaimed emissaries. I talked to a few self-appointed brand missionaries to get a deeper understanding of their perspective and experience.

For each person I interviewed, the brand served as both a mechanism for self-actualization and a symbol of identity. The brand logo was a powerful personal talisman, a message to the self. This is different from a brand having badge value, which is a message for others. While the aspirations and identities of those I spoke with varied, the role of the brand was similar. Here are a few of their stories.

Personal Transformation

"I started Spinning® when it first came out. I was in on the ground floor. Spinning seemed to touch a deep part of me; the activity was in the semi-dark where I could focus on my own effort and not those around me. I heard the instructor and the music. When I was Spinning, I began to make the connection between riding up a hill and having the grit to face problems in my life outside of the gym. Spinning fueled my personal growth and helped me become a stronger person, both physically and spiritually. This positive transformation was noticeable, even to others.

Naturally, I wanted to share this great experience with my friends. I became an instructor. I put Spinning stickers all over my jeep. Those stickers were a badge of accomplishment and achievement for me. They told others a bit about who I was (and still am—although I don't have all of those stickers anymore). I liked the logo design as well. It was really neat-looking. The interesting thing was that all of my stickers faced inward, toward me, not the outside."

—Amy B., Spinning Evangel, St. Lucie, Florida

Fraternity of Freedom Riders

My first motorcycle was a Triumph in the 1960s, but I always wanted a Harley. It's an American icon. Harley is the purest expression of freedom . . . a rejection of social norms. It's a separation from the mainstream, from everyday conformity. Riding is exhilarating. It's hard to duplicate that feeling. It is like coming home and putting on your jeans and your T-shirt. It's part of my identity. Riding is who I am, not what I do.

No other brands come close. I have never heard of a rider who rode a Harley and went to a Jap bike. There is also the H.O.G., Harley Owners Group. You are welcomed as a brother; it's a fraternity, a fellowship.

Over the years, I have bought about 30 T-shirts, boots, a riding jacket, mugs, steins, key fobs, hats, and patches. I like the slogan, "Ride to Live . . . Live to Ride." I would ride the bike even without the logo. But I can tell a Harley from any other bike. It's got a distinctive sound that warms my heart.

If my Harley were a person, it would be my girlfriend. She's attractive, exciting, and fun; we have great chemistry. And she starts all the time!

—Tom M., Harley-Davidson owner, Shelton, Connecticut

Inner Strength

I became aware of Chanel when I was a pre-teen, about 12 years old. My first Chanel item was a small handbag I purchased when I was about 25 years old. Since then, I have bought Chanel-branded nail polish, necklaces, bracelets, rings, shoes, bags, sunglasses, and clothing.

I NEVER buy knockoffs. Copycats and knockoffs diminish the value of fashion. I believe in the spirit of a brand. An authentic Chanel is not a disposable item, like so many on the market. Couture becomes a vintage item and might increase in value. Chanel is classic. My daughter might want it!

I would wear it even without the logo. It's not about showing the world I am wearing Chanel, it's about the heritage of Coco Chanel and what it means to me. She was an independent woman who defined couture in her time and is still influential today. She is an inspiring woman.

I wore a Chanel dress on my 40th birthday. I am not sure anyone knew it was Chanel, but I did. I was able to pay for that dress with my own, hard-earned money. Wearing it made me proud; it meant I had gotten to a certain point in life.

—Sonia K., Chanel fan, Atlanta, Georgia

CHAPTER 6 Recap: *Advocates and Evangels*

Influencers

- Bloggers and those with high Klout scores can be recruited as brand advocates. However, even if they have thousands of followers, these people shouldn't be treated as corporate media channels.
  - To help ensure success, brands need to get familiar with the content areas of these influential people.
  - Furthermore, brands need to make every effort to respond quickly to any inquiries these people may have.
  - Consider dedicating a resource to handle highly influential advocates.
  - Compensation may be offered as an acknowledgment of the advocate's time and effort, but not in exchange for a positive review.
- Savvy brands are tolerant of a mix of positive and negative comments. Even negative feedback generates buzz and often sales! At the very least, mixed reviews demonstrate authenticity to the reader.
  - If there are several negative comments, these should be addressed as quickly as possible.

Netizen Advocates

- Net surfing shoppers can be given incentives to advocate in exchange for value like virtual currency, coupons, or free stuff. For example, American Express offers 5,000 points for each approved referral.
  - Consumers may begin to expect rewards for advocating as a matter of course, effectively creating a new cost of doing business.

- Some advocacy programs are geared to benefit the recipient, while still giving value to the brand and carrying the endorsement of the sender. An example is the Bud Light Virtual Beer Gift on Facebook.

- Most brand rewards are structured to benefit both the giver and the receiver. This is becoming the standard. An example is the World of Warcraft Level Up for Yourself and a Friend program.

Brand Evangels

- Brand evangels, self-appointed emissaries, have aligned their identities with the values of the brand.
  - For these people, a brand serves as both a mechanism for self-actualization and a symbol of identity.
  - Evangels can't and shouldn't be bought. However, these fans may be rewarded with brand gifts and personal acknowledgment, wherever possible.

Valuing Participation

THE VALUE OF SHOPPER PARTICIPATION

Let's get back to shopper currency. Again, these behaviors are advocacy, loyalty, attention, and participation. Participation covers a lot of ground. Shoppers can participate by playing a game, scanning a code, checking into a location, scratching off a number, giving feedback, collecting things, or earning various "badges," among other activities.

Participation programs that reward behaviors have been around for quite a while. Mostly these have taken the form of promotions, contests, sweepstakes, and games. Today these programs can be much more sophisticated than in the past, because they can combine social media, virtual currency, and mobile technology, including handheld scanners and GPS.

What can marketers get out of running participation programs? Broad-scale participation or engagement programs can drive consideration. Shoppers have a set of brands in mind when considering purchase; this is called a "consideration set." While a marketer will typically reach fewer people with a game than with,

> Linking accounts is a way in which shoppers earn value. Because it is a partial surrender of personal information, it is categorized as participation. Starwood's Preferred Guest Program offered a reward to link to foursquare.
>
> *"Link your SPG and foursquare accounts to earn 250 bonus Starpoints through July 31, 2011. Plus, win Free Resort Night Awards, and more."*[1]

say, a traditional advertisement, the reverberating buzz around a hot program can make up for this. Also, in today's world, the opportunities for targeting prospects are greater than ever, given multiple access points and pass-along, viral messaging.

Digital interactivity means that participation programs are driving deeper engagement with shoppers than promotional programs in the past have done. There are several reasons for this. First, collecting box tops and entering sweepstakes were time-consuming and cumbersome activities compared to click-through entries and instantly updated standings on leader boards. Next, shoppers can play anytime, anywhere with mobile apps. Savvy marketers use this location-based capability to drive brand interaction during key occasions—in-store, at an event, or when facing an interactive billboard, for example. This makes gamified mobile promotions effective drivers of traffic as well.

Shopper marketers want deep engagement with prospects and buyers. Positive interaction with the brand keeps the brand top of mind when shoppers are planning a purchase or a store trip. Participation programs that engage shoppers are useful, because engagement increases brand consideration. This, in turn, drives sales conversion rates, as well as opportunities for upselling buyers.

Engagement can also establish brand affinity and preference. Especially in quick-turn, impulse-driven categories, engagement programs can build brand differentiation. Brands that form "fun" relationships with their shoppers—outside of the immediate realm of purchase—have extracurricular friendships with shoppers. This builds brand preference, word-of-mouth advocacy, and consideration at the point of sale.

Finally, participation programs sometimes provide a way to measure shopper responsiveness when other metrics are too difficult to obtain. Looking at when, where, and how shoppers respond to a participation program can be a proxy for brand awareness or consideration in, say, a prelaunch new product phase.

Of course, marketers want to tie engagement metrics to sales and lift. Depending on the program, drawing these correlations definitively can be challenging. However, with the increasing sophistication of tracking methods, shoppers who have identified themselves in a participation program may also be identified at the point of purchase. Of course, eliminating anonymous purchasing is one objective of a loyalty program, but even before shoppers opt into an ongoing commitment, they may surrender personal information and markers that will tag their sales later.

There are other reasons for engagement programs that don't necessarily link directly to sales volume. One is giving fodder to sales teams. Another is to create positive public relations. Engagement can activate consumers more deeply than a simple discount or "buy-get" promotion. Driving brand preference and converting shoppers is the ultimate goal.

There are a few companies that offer platforms for engaging shoppers on their mobile devices. These platforms are designed to drive brand interaction and store traffic. One of these companies is SCVNGR, based in Cambridge, Massachusetts. The following

is a description of their platform, taken from their website (http://
www.scvngr.com/).

> "SCVNGR is a game. Playing is simple: Go places. Do chal-
> lenges. Earn points! You'll unlock badges and rewards and
> share where you are and what you're up to with friends. . . .
> Rewards are awesome! They're things like free ice-cream, free
> coffee, half off pizza, 10% off your dry-cleaning, free beer and
> more! Players unlock rewards by doing challenges [approxi-
> mately six seconds per challenge] and earning points at their
> favorite places. Rewards are built by the local businesses them-
> selves and redeemed right from within the SCVNGR app."

There are many advantages to using this kind of game. First,
SCVNGR shoppers can be identified as they enter the store, or at
least before they purchase. The reason is that most of the "challenges" involve some sort of shenanigans, such as taking photos,
balancing a spoon on one's nose, or creating a tin foil origami out
of a taco wrapper. It is possible to provide incentives for trial, frequency, and cross-selling with this kind of mechanism. Also, driving store traffic alone is a good start to sales conversion and brand
preference. SCVNGR makes extensive use of gamification, but it
also overlays one's social network (via mobile).

Successful Participation

Success metrics mirror the objectives of any given program. Possible performance metrics for participation programs could
include awareness among a target audience, consideration, brand
preference, site or store traffic, depth of engagement (page views,
returning check-ins, and so on), brand personality halo, and sales
conversion.

Figure 7.1	Shopkick Rewards

Source: Shopkick.

When it comes to brick-and-mortar stores, however, almost nothing beats foot traffic for sales conversion. According to Cyriac Roeding, CEO of Shopkick, "In retail stores, foot traffic conversion rates run from about 20 percent in fashion up to about

95 percent in grocery. Conversion rates online aren't nearly as good; generally they are in the single digits. . . . As you can imagine, the conversion rate from the fitting room is even higher than simple foot traffic. Shopkick can reward shoppers for trying on clothes [in the fitting room]."

Shopkick (http://www.shopkick.com/) is one of the most firmly established players in the mobile engagement space for commercial enterprise (see Figure 7.1 and Figure 7.2). I spoke with Shopkick's CEO to learn why the company has been so successful in the space.

INTERVIEW WITH CYRIAC ROEDING, SHOPKICK COFOUNDER AND CHIEF EXECUTIVE OFFICER

Cyriac Roeding is cofounder and chief executive officer at Shopkick, Inc. Before Shopkick, Cyriac was founder and executive vice president of CBS Mobile, where he launched CBS Corporation's (NYSE: CBS) mobile businesses across CBS Entertainment, CBS Sports, CBS News, and the CW Network. Previously, Cyriac also

| Figure 7.2 | **Shopkick Logo** |

served as cofounder at 12snap, a European mobile marketing and entertainment company, and developed growth strategies at McKinsey & Company.

Cyriac earned his MA in engineering and business administration from Germany's Technical University of Karlsruhe, where he graduated summa cum laude. He also studied Japanese management at Sophia University in Tokyo. Cyriac has received several industry honors, including the first Lion Awards for mobile concepts at the Cannes Lion Festival in France (in 2003 and 2004). In 2007 and 2008, Cyriac and his team received the only Emmy Award nominations for mobile. For 2007, he was elected as global and North American chairman of the Mobile Marketing Association, with 600 member companies worldwide.

Q: What makes Shopkick an enticing business proposition for companies?

A: *The reason retailers and brands use Shopkick is simple: we are driving the number one success metric for conversion: foot traffic. In retail stores, foot traffic conversion rates run from about 20 percent in fashion up to about 95 percent in grocery. Conversion rates online aren't nearly as good; generally they are in the single digits.*

So, if foot traffic is so important, why doesn't anyone reward you for coming into the store? The answer is that no one has a clue that you are there. It is only when you are leaving the store that you lose your anonymity. And at that point, the basket is already full, and the shopping trip is over. Obviously, that is not the perfect time to greet a shopper.

Shopkick rewards people for coming into the store and then tempts them with great offers. Right now, nobody else has the technology to know you are there, but Shopkick does. GPS is imprecise. GPS has a range of about 500 yards on cellphones; you can't know if the shopper is standing in the parking lot or in the store next door.

The Shopkick in-store device emits an inaudible signal, which is set so that the microphone in your smartphone can pick it up and decode the signal. That code shows exactly where the shopper is standing. This technology is also very easy for shop owners to acquire and use. It is only about $100 per unit—just plug it in! Many national retailers are participating, including Best Buy, Macy's, Simon Malls, Sports Authority, Wet Seal, and now Toys 'R' Us, just in time for the holidays.

Q: What activities can shoppers engage in, in order to earn kicks?

A: *Shopkick is the first reward program for desired shopper behaviors. Shoppers can be rewarded for scanning items, walking into a store, and even walking around to different areas within the store. For example, shoppers can earn extra kicks for visiting the gaming department of Best Buy. At American Eagle, shoppers are rewarded for trying on clothes and being in the fitting room. As you can imagine, the conversion rate from the fitting room is even higher than that from simple foot traffic. Shopkick can reward shoppers for trying on clothes. We are also testing a new program that rewards shoppers for buying items.*

Q: Will Shopkick incorporate more gamification?

A: *Yes. We have a number of advisors on our board who are experts in gaming and electronics. Our advisors include founders and principals at Electronic Arts, Zynga, LinkedIn, and other groundbreaking digital companies.*

In the future, Shopkick shoppers will get bonuses in games. We'll see more of that kind of thing happening in Shopkick.

Q: Can shoppers get kicks for entering a store online?

A: *They can't today. But that is not excluded for tomorrow.*

Q: What does Shopkick do that nothing else can?

A: *Let's look at Shopkick, SCVNGR, and foursquare. There is something different at the heart of each of these platforms. Shopkick is a location-based shopping app. Shopping is at the heart of our app. Next, there are location-based social apps like foursquare and Facebook Places. Finally, there are games and location-based games like SCVNGR. A game is at the heart of that app.*

Today, each party is dabbling in the others' territory. However, each app is grounded in a different area. If you launch an app and you want to go shopping, which one will you launch? You will launch a shopping app. To leap from social to shopping is a big leap, and also very indirect. On the other hand, if your core thing is a game, that is far from shopping, too.

We want to be the best location-based shopping app in the world. That is where the biggest business proposition sits.

Q: Do you think the market is moving toward a universal virtual currency?

A: *Yes—It's kicks!! That's why we started it!*

Shopkick offers the most universal currency in the U.S. market today. The kicks currency is redeemable across retailers in America; you can earn kicks at one retailer and redeem them at another. Consumers love to spend wherever they choose. They don't like to be restricted to one place. This is a coalition model, similar to Nectar in the United Kingdom or PAYBACK in Germany. This is the only one in the United

States. It is unlikely that a retailer will join other coalitions once it is already in a program, such as ours.

It is also unlikely that Facebook Credits will be a universal currency in the future. The reason is that it's not easily integrated into retail businesses. Are retailers interested in giving up their customer relationships to Facebook?

In terms of Facebook Credits and Google currencies, these work well as online currencies, but they don't translate well into offline currency. The leap from online to offline is very large. I don't want to shop with Facebook at Macy's. I want to shop with a shopping app, like Shopkick.

Q: What is your vision for marketing in the next five years?

A: *We will be closer to the consumer, understanding the consumer better than ever. Also, we'll close the loop with the retailers.*

Marketing itself is moving toward a 100 percent performance-based platform. If you invest a dollar in the left column, do you get a dollar back on the other side? This is the criterion for success. In the future, marketing will have an impact when it can be measured; then the results will speak for themselves.

Marketers need to bring the fun back into shopping. A satisfying experience for the consumer is one that is shopper-centric. It doesn't annoy the shopper with unnecessary stuff. An unsatisfying experience is commercial-centric. It is geared toward someone else's benefit and is not simple to use. Shoppers like experiences that are simple, fun, and rewarding.

This is our first-year anniversary; we are shocked at how well Shopkick has been received. Today we have more than 2.2 million users and the largest number of participating retailers of any program in the United States.

Mobile games like SCVNR and Shopkick aren't the only ways to drive store traffic with value exchanges. Zynga's smash hit games, like FarmVille and Mafia Wars, have attracted a large and diverse audience that is motivated to take the game into retail environments. In 2010, Zynga partnered with the retail chain 7-Eleven to reward game players who visit the convenience stores. Virtual currency and goods were rewarded within the game. The next section gives a summary of the case, an interview with 7-Eleven's senior digital and loyalty manager, and an interview with a player who participated in the campaign.

INTERVIEW WITH EVAN BRODY, SENIOR MARKETING MANAGER—DIGITAL AND LOYALTY, 7-ELEVEN

Q: I understand that the promotion was a great success. How did shop managers feel about it?

A: *Franchisees and store managers were very happy to see excited customers coming into their stores searching for Zynga-related products. For me, the best story was when I went to a launch event at one of our Dallas stores and met two FarmVille players who were neighbors in the game but had not met in real life until that day. They had both driven several hundred miles to come to the store to buy products and meet. It was also great to talk to guests who were purchasing large quantities of products to share with their friends who were not able to make it to a store.*

Q: What was the feedback from shoppers?

A: *Guests loved the program. Since different products contained different in-game gifts, customers learned about products like fresh-cut fruit, which they did not even know 7-Eleven stores carried.*

Case Study | ZYGNA and 7-Eleven

Program Background and Objectives

The recession hurt most retail businesses, and convenience stores were no exception. By 2010, most convenience store shoppers were buying either coffee and donuts or energy drinks, but bypassing the other food offerings. Consumers weren't considering 7-Eleven for meals. In fact, sales were flagging in several food categories, from fresh fruit to hot foods.

7-Eleven needed to expand the number of categories bought in-store and drive consideration in the shopper's mind. Further, the brand wanted to draw traffic from some new demographics, to grow its appeal.

Finally, 7-Eleven needed to keep the brand's profile of fun and popular tie-ins (Simpson's Kwik-E-Mart, Transformers, and so on), while delivering differentiation and engagement.

How It Worked

From June 1 through July 15, 2010, 7-Eleven shoppers could buy any of 30 different, specially marked private label products that featured codes redeemable in Zynga games. The products included ice cream, Slurpee, Big Gulp, and other signature products. These products had limited-edition packaging that was tied to Zynga games. More than 7,000 retail stores participated.

The codes were redeemable for exclusive virtual goods in FarmVille, Mafia Wars, or YoVille. Codes could be redeemed at BuyEarnPlay.com during the promotional period.

Consumers also had the opportunity to earn an "über gift" in each game by buying qualified products and completing a designated task in the game.

> **Results**
>
> *More than 1 million users registered on the website and nearly 3.3 million codes were entered. In total, 77.6% of registered users (818,753 people) entered codes for multiple products. Measured brand consideration increased 6 percentage points within targeted audiences.[2]*

Q: Who played this game? Did it pull new demographic traffic into your stores?

A: *The guests who participated in the program were similar to the demographics of those playing the three Zynga games. We saw a skew during the promotion toward older females, which is not typical for our stores.*

Q: What surprised you the most about this promotion?

A: *The most surprising thing was the speed at which it spread. Typically with a new promotion, it takes a few days or a week for excitement to build, but with this program, guests were already looking for products before the program officially launched. Zynga players are extremely passionate about the games and were very excited to have this real-world extension.*

Q: How do games like this help set 7-Eleven apart from the competition?

A: *It shows that 7-Eleven is more than just your typical convenience store. We are partnering with properties that our guests love and offering them unique and exclusive products.*

For 7-Eleven, it is about setting our company apart and doing things that no one else does. We are uniquely positioned, with our stores and our different proprietary products, like Slurpee drinks, to transform the shopping experience each month.

Fun is very important and a driver for our programs. We want to be not only a convenient destination, but someplace you enjoy going to every day.

To get a sense of the experience of playing FarmVille (http://www.farmville.com/) and engaging in the 7-Eleven program, I spoke with Beth J. She talked about her motivations for playing and how the engagement with the 7-Eleven worked for her.

INTERVIEW WITH BETH J., FARMVILLE DENIZEN, SWARTHMORE, PENNSYLVANIA

Q: When did you start playing FarmVille?

A: *I met some people from Australia on a cruise, and we became friends. My friend Ruth from this trip—she begged me to play. I said, okay, but I need all of your friends to play with, because I don't know anyone on the game. That was two years ago. But now all my friends are playing and my friends' friends . . . but Ruth and her friends stopped playing!*

Q: When do you play?

A: *I spend about an hour a day doing it—right before bed, about midnight to 1 a.m. There is a certain group who plays at this time, and I play with people from Europe, too. The time has come out of my sleep. I used to sleep about eight hours a night, and now I sleep about seven.*

I got a phone that doesn't carry the game, in order to avoid having FarmVille always available. I know I would end up playing it on the phone. That's why I didn't get it. I want to control it and keep it to a minimum. It's not healthy to do too much.

I keep myself down to one game. It's easy to get sucked into other ones. Zynga wants you to play all of its games. For example, you can take your FarmVille stuff and send it to CityVille. . . . There is a constant temptation to link into other games. But you can also opt out and block.

Q: Why do you do it? What's the most enjoyable thing about playing?

A: *It's a mindless, relaxing thing . . . that's why I play it late at night. You can kind of zone out and do it. I am into decorating, and I had dollhouses as a girl . . . it's like playing with dollhouses. You can decorate and arrange things and create an environment.*

It's also about the friends you make. It's a fun social thing. I pick up a bunch of friends and their friends. For example, there is Sonia in St. Louis—I've never met her, but she is so sweet. I play with about 50 Facebook friends—I try to keep it at about 50, which is low. People who are doing this are posting pictures and comments . . . you learn about them and their lives. I have gotten to know people in my community just through the game. I started playing with some people I sort of know, like Jackie in town. But now we are really friends!

Everyone plays it differently. Jackie is the most competitive person I know; she has to have all of the trees. I am into getting the most mastery points. Then I think—what if I get all of the mastery points? I won't have any goals left.

Q: Who plays?

A: *There are no young kids in our group—they don't have the stamina!! These are people in their forties and fifties. There are many more women than men. Sometimes the women play for their husbands, just to be able to send themselves stuff. I know one woman who gave her husband an entirely pink farm.*

Q: What about buying things in the game?

A: *I buy FarmVille cash only at the grocery store, because it keeps my purchasing to a minimum. I don't use my credit card to buy online because it's too easy!!! You think the $10 doesn't add up—but it does!!*

I have friends who say part of their fun is to avoid spending any money . . . but I put it into my entertainment budget. I like to buy Facebook cash, because once you convert it to FarmVille cash, it's too easy to spend it.

Q: Can you buy things in the game without using your credit card?

A: *Well, there's land expansion. You can expand for 120 FarmVille cash. But Zynga seems to extract all the cash it can from those who will pay, so after that, you need 10 neighbors and some coins you have earned yourself in order to expand.*

Also, I do watch the ads to earn FarmVille cash. After the advertisement—at the end—it says you have earned your FarmVille cash. There is a link to the website for the merchandise, but you don't have to click it to earn the FarmVille cash.

I really like it—because it's "free" FarmVille cash. It's not costing me out of pocket. I watch the ads as often as I can. I have also seen a Farmer's Insurance Blimp in the game.

Another way to earn is with the Capital One Statue. The Capital One Statue lets you quadruple the yield from your crops. It's a real incentive to put the statue there. But I do try to hide the statue a little. Meantime, I stared at it for a full week.

Q: How many of the 7-Eleven items did you buy?

A: *I bought all the things at the store—the Slurpee, the ice cream, the bottle of water, and the sandwich. . . . The FarmVille promotion was the first time I went into a 7-Eleven. . . . I liked the rewards. They were really cute, like a water slide for a sheep! It was fun.*

While the Zynga 7-Eleven program represents a new way to reward behaviors, engaging shoppers in games, contests, and other programs is nothing new. I spoke with longtime industry expert Keith Simmons, CEO of PrizeLogic, about how the world of shopper engagement is changing.

INTERVIEW WITH KEITH SIMMONS, CEO, PRIZELOGIC

A veteran of online promotions, Keith Simmons served as one of the principals of ePrize from 2002 to 2006, leading its business expansion. Prior to promotions, Keith's career in media sales and management spanned 20 years at Turner Broadcasting, Court TV, MTV, WDIV, NBC Detroit, and WJLA, ABC Washington, DC.

Q: What strategic reasons do companies have for using sweepstakes, mobile games, contests, and instant-win games?

A: *In the beginning, companies wanted customers to sign up for their promotions and loyalty programs. It was about customer acquisition and building a database. They wanted data.*

Now it's much more sales-driven, and the promotion is the differentiator. Today, Facebook "likes" is the new metric. It's like a big land grab in Facebook. The reason companies are doing this is because likes help make their advertising more effective. People are more likely to click a banner ad because their friends are fans of that page. Fans beget more fans.

Q: Is there any research, beyond vendor studies, that shows that fans translate to higher conversion rates?

A: *I haven't seen it yet. The first public study will probably be a Procter & Gamble or Unilever case. Or Facebook could commission a study to show the relationship between likes and sales. But Facebook is only one of 25 things that brands need to do to maintain their media presence.*

Consumers are using their mobile devices to access the web as well as Facebook. Previously, consumers used their computers. But on the mobile, apps and ads don't show up very well. Facebook has to learn how to get sponsored messages at those mobile access points. It's a skinny space.

Q: We agree that user experience makes or breaks a program and ultimately a brand. What makes for a satisfying user experience?

A: *Instant gratification is satisfying. Therefore, immediate feedback is important. We did a promotion with an A test cell and a B test cell. In the A cell, you enter now and wait to see if you won tickets to the Super Bowl. In the B cell, you enter now and instantly see if you have won a T-shirt. The T-shirts won in terms of response, even though they were of lesser value, because the feedback was instant. As an industry veteran, I believe in instant gratification.*

The total experience needs to be easy to be satisfying. You have about seven fields to ask before you face abandonment. More than seven questions take too much time.

Q: Why do shoppers like games? What motivates them?

A: *Game participants always skew female, usually ages 20 to 54. The fastest-growing segment of game growth is among moms. It's "me time" and hobbylike. In fact, a male-oriented promotion still skews female. In these games, it is a low-cost way that anyone can play. It's like a chance to win the lottery, but without paying for a ticket.*

> *Besides tripling your opt-in rate over a typical sweepstakes, instant win promotions boast an average of 4 to 7 times return frequency with an average of 2.5 to 4 minutes spent on your site."[3]*

Now there's another phenomenon, too—a community of sweep-stakes hobbyists. This is what they do in their spare time for fun. There are about 25 to 30,000 sweepstakes hobbyists. We could put a test pattern up and still get 30,000 people. But brands aren't trying to market to those people; they aren't prospects.

The question is how to get to the real prospects. The more brands can control this, the better the conversion will be. Prospects can be buyers who notice a code on-pack, or they can come from a database or point-of-sale ad.

In quick-serve restaurants (QSR), we give them their first entry free. It's an ad with a code or a banner ad on Facebook. This casts a wide net for the promotion. The free code is the first engagement. If the person likes it, they buy the product. The paid code is the second engagement. Roughly a quarter of the people will buy the product, using PrizeLogic's numbers. We have a few clients with the same results. Part of the success of this is that it works on a fast purchase cycle. This kind of program would work in a convenience store as well. Of course the Zynga 7-Eleven promotion stands out as an example.

Q: What is the role of social media in branded games and sweeps?

A: *It's friends referring friends. Brands will need that base to get engagement.*

Social media are great tools, but they are sometimes used as a forum for bitching about a brand. Companies that want to keep their page positive run promotions. This is content that can keep people engaged in a positive way with the brand. Also, companies can move the negative comments down the page, so they're not the first thing you see.

Q: What is the role of mobile in gaming?

A: *Mobile combines digital interactivity with brick-and-mortar experience. For example, if you are ordering a sandwich at SUBWAY, you are standing in front of the sandwich assembly line. While waiting, you can play an instant-win game by scanning a free QR code, which is on a display card. Before you even order your bread, you have registered and played.*

Now if you go to the beverage station and buy a drink, the cup has a code on it too. You can enter that code and play again. You have played twice before you leave the store. This is immediate gratification that is embedded in the in-store experience. Customers are participating in the total brand experience, registering their information, and having fun.

Q: What is your vision for gamification in the next five years?

A: *Games will be increasingly personalized to your groups of friends, not national platforms. We will see more social gaming, where you are playing against or with your friends. There will be more leader boards where you have picked your opponents, and fewer national leader boards.*

At PrizeLogic, we ran a game for a client that asked the question, "Are you the big gamer on campus?" This ad performed okay. But when we added a personal dimension, we got a much better response.

The challenge got more specific and personally relevant: "Are you the big gamer at NYU?" "Are you the big gamer at Michigan?" and so forth. We got this information from Facebook. This shift changed the media execution. As the participants played the game, their leader board was against their group on campus only. The college-specific ad had 25 percent better media performance than the generic ad. Here the key performance indexes are the click-through rates and abandonment percentages.

In the next few years, the most successful brands won't be running national, one-size-fits-all games. Instead, there will be more customized content for people to play with their friends. The brand experience is now a personal experience. It is always relevant if it is personal.

CHAPTER 7 Recap: *Valuing Participation*

Participation

- Participation covers a lot of ground. Shoppers can participate by playing a game, scanning a code, checking into a location, scratching off a number, giving feedback, collecting things, or earning various "badges," among other activities.

  Participation programs are strategic, because engagement can drive:
  - Brand consideration
  - Foot traffic
  - Sales conversion rates
  - Opportunities for upselling
  - Brand preference and affinity
  - Positive PR halo
- Participation programs can also be a way to measure shopper responsiveness when other metrics are too difficult to obtain.

Successful Participation Programs

- Get immediate. Instant gratification is satisfying.

  Lesser-value "instant win" games are more fun than greater-value wait-and-see prizes. We did a promotion with an A test cell and a B test cell. In the A cell, you enter now and wait to see if you have won tickets to the Super Bowl. In the B cell, you enter now and instantly see if you have won a T-shirt. The T-shirts won in terms of response, even though they were of lesser value, because the feedback was instant.
- Get personal. Personal interests, a social graph, and geography keep programming relevant.

- PrizeLogic ran a game for a client that asked the question, "Are you the big gamer on campus?" This ad performed okay. But when we added a personal dimension, we got a much better response.
- Keep it simple.

The Product as Souvenir

LABOR MARKET FOR SHOPPING TASKS

As we have seen, there are a growing number of opportunities to earn value by performing shopping tasks, such as watching ads, walking into stores, scanning products, signing up for a membership program, or even linking membership programs. What are the motivations for participation?

Many shoppers are ready to work for the rewards themselves, which would be beyond their ability or willingness to pay for with cash. Earning points through various activities feels like getting something for "free." Most shoppers don't consciously recognize their time and effort as being equivalent to money. Here is a typical sentiment among people who are willing to earn points:

> I do watch the ads to earn FarmVille cash. After the advertisement—at the end—it says you have earned your FarmVille cash. . . . I really like it because it's free FarmVille cash!
>
> —Beth J., FarmVille denizen

Beth considers the FarmVille cash "free" because her labor isn't actual money. Her time and energy are coming out of a different account (time), not her bank account (cash). And for many people, that makes all the difference. This brings us to the concept of "mental accounting." Richard Thaler has written about mental accounting in *Marketing Science* magazine: "Mr. S admires a $125 cashmere sweater at the department store. He declines to buy it feeling that it is too extravagant. Later that month, he receives the same sweater from his wife for a birthday present. He is very happy. Mr. and Mrs. S have only joint bank accounts."[1]

Shoppers have various mental accounts from which they spend. Indulgent items, like the cashmere sweater, are "forbidden fruit" for shoppers who are looking to exert self-control in everyday expenditures. This is especially true during a recession. However, when the price comes out of a *different mental budget* (here, gifts), the expenditure is acceptable.

Performing labor in return for scrip is popular in economic hard times. A combination of technology and the recession have turbocharged the shoppers' labor market. In fact, from 2008 to 2010, there was a 16 percent increase in shopper participation in points programs.[2] Most experts agree that these shopper behaviors are here to stay.

Labor-for-scrip programs are also popular among people who have difficulty earning in the "regular" labor market, such as housewives in the 1960s who were collecting Green Stamps that could be redeemed for merchandise in a catalog.

The rewards feel "free" because labor isn't cash; therefore, scrip feels like "found money." It doesn't fit within the shopper's regular budget, but lies in a separate mental account designated for treats and extras, and for bigger-ticket items as well.

One such bigger-ticket item is a child's college education. The example of the Couponing to Disney Program, which enables

S&H Green Stamps

S&H Green Stamps were introduced in 1896. Green Stamps were one of the first loyalty programs in the United States. They were so popular by 1964 that S&H printed three times as many stamps as the U.S. Post Office.[3]

> *Whenever you went to the department store, grocery store, or appliance store, you got Green Stamps. You had to put them into books to collect and redeem them. You sent in your stamps for things in the printed catalog. They had redemption centers too—you could walk into the redemption store and get a TV, record player, radio, and other good things.*
>
> *There was a great deal of enthusiasm among the women about Green Stamps. My aunts and my mom would get excited, and they would talk about it: how many books of stamps they had; what they were going to get. These women didn't have too many ways to earn money. Green Stamps was a way to earn things on your own and get things you wanted without dipping into the household budget and without a husband's approval. It was butter and egg money—it was her own budget.*
>
> —Marcia H., Green Stamps buyer,
> Swarthmore, Pennsylvania

gatekeeper moms to earn points toward a trip to Disney, is a perfect case in point. A bank's save-the-change program, which rounds purchase prices up to the nearest dollar and deposits the change in the shopper's savings account, works similarly. In these cases, rewards are symbols of savvy; the products are trophies for effort and smarts. Particularly in a recessionary environment, these kinds of programs allow ways for cash-strapped people to leverage another asset—their time.

LOOK MA—NO HANDS!

While there is plenty of motivation to work for the rewards them-selves, another impetus to labor is that the work feels like fun, not toil. This is where gamification comes into play. Blogger Om Malik recounted his feelings about foursquare in 2009 this way:

> If you follow me on Twitter, then you're already aware of my obsession with foursquare, a New York–based service that taps into the narcissistic appeal of being able to post unusual loca-tions such as our office cafeteria, Chatz Cafe, or best recom-mendations about a place and marries it to social networking. What's more fun—it all seems like a game.[4]

By May 2011, foursquare was overtaken by Facebook Places as the most popular location-based social network in the United States. According to an article in *Techland*, "90% of respondents actively using check-in apps said they use Facebook Places."[5]

People who love location-based services feel that they are fun because of the badges, but especially because of the social network-ing aspects of the "game." However, many Americans don't feel that these services offer enough "fun" or other value to get them to participate. What is the biggest hurdle? Privacy concerns, accord-ing to a survey by the digital agency Beyond.[6] Respondents who did indicate interest in participating would share their location in exchange for a discount; 40 percent of those who have never checked in said that they would consider sharing their location with Groupon. However, only 21 percent said that they would share their location for a status badge.

Be that as it may, Om Malik and apparently many, many others do enjoy social geo-check in. In June 2011, foursquare announced that it had passed the 10 million mark. Much of foursquare's success seems to be coming from global markets, beyond North America.

How can we explain this? One man's fun is another man's privacy concern. According to the Pew Internet & American Life Project, "61% [of adults] do not feel compelled to limit the amount of information that can be found about them online . . . [however,] 38% say they have taken steps to limit the amount of online information that is available about them."[7] Nearly 40 percent of people feel concerned enough to have taken action to protect themselves. If that number holds over time (a big "if"), location-based social networks and other platforms may need to offer increased privacy to improve participation, or risk the possibility that a large percentage of the population won't opt in.

An indication that this may be happening is the advent of Google+, whose selling point is the user's ability to draw circles around groups of friends and exclude others. According to Google+'s website, "You share different things with different people. But sharing the right stuff with the right people shouldn't be a hassle. Circles makes it easy to put your friends from Saturday night in one circle, your parents in another, and your boss in a circle by himself, just like real life."[8] The implication for marketers is that advocacy could be limited to the shopper's immediate cohorts. This means that resharing becomes critically important to using the shopper as a media channel.

Getting back to shopper currency, fun is fun. "Labor" can have real entertainment value for participants, beyond the reward itself. Promotions provide easy examples. For instance, in early 2011, Pop Secret ran a social media campaign leveraging the movie awards season. The goal of the program was to associate Pop Secret with movie-watching occasions at home and drive incremental merchandising and sales. Consumers had a chance to go online to write and direct a short movie scene starring Pop Secret's Kernel characters—directly from their national campaign. Users could select backgrounds, write dialogue, and post their completed movies on YouTube or forward them to friends.

Randomly chosen entries won instant prizes. Pop Secret "swag bags" were given away during a Twitter party on Academy Awards night. The grand prize included an at-home 3D multimedia center. All in all, more than 84,000 user-generated videos were made. What made the program successful? It was fun.[9]

While the Pop Secret movie game was fun, it rewarded participants with a chance to win. On the other hand, Zynga rewards game players with digital scrip. Games such as FarmVille and CityVille, with in-game advertising and retailer tie-ins, are examples of games that exchange shopper currencies for virtual currency. Smart brands are getting in on the ground floor of gaming. According to a report in eMarketer, "Nearly 62 million US internet users, or 27% of the online audience, will play at least one game on a social network monthly this year [2011], up from 53 million in 2010."[10]

Games are on the rise and may represent one of the best ways to provide incentives for behaviors. In the same report, eMarketer noted that revenues from virtual goods will outstrip revenues from in-game ads and lead generation, proving the point that game behavior is at the heart of motivation. "Revenues from virtual goods make up the majority of overall social gaming revenues, accounting for $510 million in revenues in 2010. eMarketer estimates social gaming sites will earn $653 million in virtual goods revenues this year, compared to just $192 million in ad revenues and $248 million in lead-generation offers."[11] The point is this: gamers are motivated by virtual goods because they are part of the fun. And pursuing fun is one of the best incentives for shopper currencies, like attention and participation.

WHERE IS THE BRAND?

While all of this shopper participation is exciting and even profitable, what is the role of the product? What happens to branding?

As shoppers become the new media channel, the product becomes the souvenir of their experience. And the experience is branding.

Consider this in-game ad. Capital One financial services ran an interactive ad in FarmVille. FarmVille denizens could choose to put a statue of Capital One on their farm for one week. In exchange for their attention to this digital billboard, Capital One would allow the yield of players' crops to increase. This is a quintessential shopper economy exchange: attention for scrip.

I interviewed a FarmVille player about this program. She reported, "The Capital One Statue lets you quadruple the yield from your crops. It's a real incentive to put the statue there."

The branding is embedded in the experience: the crops yield much more with Capital One. This is perfectly on message for Capital One's brand. The bank's website touts its brand benefits, which dovetail with the FarmVille ad, "Earn 3x More on Your Savings."[12]

The role of the product changes in the shopper economy. When shoppers are laboring for value, the labor becomes more central to the branding experience than a simple payment of cash would. The product then becomes a souvenir of the experience.

Consider the work required to earn the SPINsider badge on foursquare at the SXSW Conference. Participants needed to see one band from a list of 35 "Must-Hear Acts" recommended by *SPIN* magazine and check in to foursquare while at the venue. This unlocked one SPINsider badge. The benefit from the badge (beyond social status) was the opportunity to be one of the first five people to present the badge and gain free admission to a concert. Advocacy was also built into the program. Participants who set up a group of SXSW friends on foursquare were entered to win a chance for the whole crew to get passes and VIP upgrades at the venue.

SPIN magazine created a branded experience at the SXSW conference using foursquare as a platform. The editors of *SPIN* became curators and guides for people who enjoy music. Followers were rewarded with goodies. *SPIN* magazine itself communicates across media, including the hard-copy magazine, iPad app, and website, as well as having an interactive presence at many music

SPINsider BADGE on Foursquare

SXSW Conference, 2011

1. *Follow SPIN on foursquare.*
2. *Go see one band from our 35 Must-Hear Acts preview. Don't forget to check in to foursquare when you're there.*
   You can also add bands to your foursquare "To Do" list, directly from our preview.
3. *This will unlock the SPINsider badge.*
4. *Be one of the first 5 people each day on $3/17$ and $3/18$ to present the SPINsider badge at the SPIN Oxygen Lounge on 313½ East 6th Street, from 12 – 6pm.*

To make it even easier, we can send you reminders when these 35 Bands are about to take the stage. Just set up a group with you and your SXSW friends on GroupMe, and opt in for reminders. We'll even pick one group at random and give you and your whole crew SPIN@Stubb's passes with VIP upgrades! Let SPIN's Editors be your guide to the best of SXSW.[13]

festivals and concerts. If a reader or listener logs onto *SPIN* or picks up a magazine, this becomes a concrete connection to those memories and that brand experience.

Experiential marketing isn't new, and it isn't confined to content providers like *SPIN*. Charmin toilet paper hosted a temporary potty stop in Times Square during the 2010 holiday season to showcase its product and, more important, its brand. The brand took advantage of the lack of public facilities in Times Square and created a Charmin experience.[14]

While the Charmin restroom did not use digital scrip to reward shopper behavior, it was an example of experiential branding. Experiential branding must be *the new normal* as brands and retailers increasingly compensate shoppers for behavior.

EXPERIENCE DESIGN

As the labor market for shopper behavior expands, experience design (XD) will become an increasingly important discipline for marketers. While shoppers are working to earn value, their labor becomes part of the branding experience. Therefore, XD must be at the forefront of branding.

What is XD? "Experience design (XD) is the practice of designing products, processes, services, events, and environments with a focus placed on the quality of the user experience and culturally relevant solutions, with less emphasis placed on increasing and improving functionality of the design."[15]

Nathan Shedroff is one of the leading thinkers in this discipline. Shedroff offers an approach to designing meaningful experiences in his book *Making Meaning* and on his website, Nathan .com. He describes six dimensions of experience:

1. Significance (function/performance, and so on)

2. Breadth (product, brand, channel)

3. Intensity (engagement)

4. Duration (time)

5. Triggers (senses and symbols)

6. Interaction (passive or interactive)

Historically, brand managers have sought to control the four Ps: product, price, placement, and promotion. These have been variously modified over the years to include different aspects of marketing, including adding the Ps of purpose (cause marketing and vision), people, and process, among others. Nevertheless, most of these additional Ps fall under the second dimension of experience, breadth.

Nathan Shedroff points out that to create and manage a customer's experience, an expanded list of elements must be controlled, including the intensity of the experience, its duration, sensorial triggers, and the nature of the interaction. These elements have become more important as digital marketing has taken off. The reason is that technology allows brands to act as an interface to the world beyond the store.

Think about the possibilities for brand interfaces using a Google Goggles–type technology. Google Goggles is a mobile technology that allows the user to take a photo of something and get information about that item. For example, a picture of a famous painting will yield the artist's name, the date the picture was painted, and more information. A picture of a published book will yield information about the author and publisher, as well as an opportunity to purchase the book with a click. Intriguingly, pictures of physical landmarks such as the Brooklyn Bridge will yield a list of search results, too.[16]

If a brand were to employ this visual search technology, imagine how the experience could create feelings, relationship, and meaning for the user. For instance, today REI offers an app that lists ski resorts, reports the weather at those locations, and provides trail maps of the resorts. Imagine that in addition to that, a user could take a picture of a mountain (say, from a car window) and get information about its elevation, trails, and history, and when the next REI trip to that mountain will take place. Or in another example, Sotheby's could offer more than upcoming auctions and catalogs on its app. Users could take a picture of something at a flea market, estate sale, or country auction and get some rudimentary information about the object. This might work especially well for certain categories, like porcelain, vintage wine, guns, and architecture (Sotheby's Real Estate). These are just a few simple ways in which a brand can create a lens through which the world can be interpreted and experienced. These kinds of experiences can foster a relationship between the user and the brand that extends beyond the product and the store.

In 1999, Pine and Gilmore published the thought-provoking book *The Experience Economy*. While many things have changed since that book was written, several important concepts were prescient. "The transition to an economy in which experiences fuel the engine of growth will undergo many of the same changes encountered in the earlier transition from the Industrial to the Service Economy. The transition begins when companies give away experiences in order to sell existing offerings better. . . . Theme-based restaurants, for example, still charge for the food when customers come in for the experience."[17] This example certainly extends to a place like Starbucks, which offers much more than simply a cup of coffee.

But beyond the store as theater idea, with today's technology, it's possible to create a branded filter through which to experience the world. Furthermore, shopper currencies enable brands to sell experiences to shoppers in exchange for behaviors, such as participation or advocacy. Pine and Gilmore encouraged readers, "In business to business situations, stage experiences where customers pay you to sell to them."[18] This is exactly what is happening today. Because shoppers are the new medium, they are marketers' business partners. Through their behavior, like shopper participation in the 7-Eleven FarmVille game, shoppers are paying brands to sell to them. Shopper/players buy products with codes at a retailer to get rewarded in a game, which in turn sells them more product.

DO WE NEED A CXO?

Several big insurance agencies, such as USAA, Cigna, and Allstate, and retailers like Dunkin' Donuts have appointed a chief experience officer (CXO).

What is a CXO? This person is in charge of the customer experience, from soup to nuts. This role consolidates all of the backroom operations, such as claims, menu selection, and fulfillment, that have front-of-the-house visibility. In the past, customer satisfaction or creating a good customer experience was often "everyone's job." However, this usually meant that everyone thought someone else was doing it, and the customer was lost in the shuffle. In other firms, the customer experience was the CEO's job. But CEOs perform numerous other functions for the company and its employees, and these rarely left enough time to perform well in this detail-oriented job. To remedy this, several companies are simply assigning someone to the task. This person needs to

NRF: Disney Realizes Product Isn't Everything

"While Mr. Finney [Stephen Finney, SVP, global retail operations, Disney Store] contends Disney consumer products are by far the most successful licensing business worldwide—whether measuring market share, ROI, or product-development programs—a strategy of simply sticking product in stores failed . . .

Embracing a mantra, "Best 30 minutes of a child's day," a team of 220 worked two years on bringing the "Magic" of its theme parks to retail. Among the "hero fixtures" are a station where kids can assemble cars from the Disney-Pixar "Cars" movie, a Magic Mirror in which girls can summon their favorite princess with a wand, and Magical Trees programmable with changing colors and images."[19]

understand the 360-degree customer experience—from awareness through experience to lasting impression.

Rick Nash from RetailCustomerExperience.com wrote this about the emerging CXO role: "Customer experience investments are building momentum as the power to decide how and when a consumer interacts with a company has shifted to the consumer. Companies need to adapt and change their view from the inside out, to outside in. This will likely pose a daunting challenge to organizations; appointing a CXO is simply the first step."[20]

Shoppers choose to advocate or participate in branded activities for value, which usually includes both hard and soft rewards. This means that there could be an element of fun in advocating for a brand (not merely getting the "free" Groupon for three friends' purchases). The entertainment or informational aspect is an opportunity for branding. Let's say a Groupon advocate is working to recruit three friends to buy a spa facial. The hard reward is the "free" facial for the advocate. The soft reward may be a downloadable iTunes sound track of falling rain, the kind that is played in the spa. Or perhaps the advocate is given special customized invitations to send out. These invitations could take an uploaded photo and do a mini-makeover on the shopper's face, showing a before-and-after visual of the person. This softer experience can be fun, personal, persuasive, and branded. You can bundle group packages for weddings or proms, using Groupon, and reward the biggest group with a free limo to the event. The nature of the experience should reflect the values and personality of the brand.

Let's take the Disney example from the sidebar. What if a harder currency exchange had been coupled with the softer reward of play value? Children and their parents could earn points, as in Shopkick or CheckPoints, for scanning codes or taking pictures. What if the pictures were of an in-store puppet show with Disney characters, or if the scanned code was located at the bottom of a sunken treasure chest? These points could accumulate to become redeemable discounts for product or for privileges within the store or at the theme park. These are ways to exchange shopper behavioral currencies for virtual goods, and ultimately for profits.

The art of creating shopper experiences is increasingly sophisticated. Ken Nisch, an award-winning retail architect, spoke with me about how these experiences are changing and what the future may look like.

INTERVIEW WITH KEN NISCH, ARCHITECT AND CHAIRMAN, JGA RETAIL DESIGN (HTTP://WWW.JGA.COM/)

Since 1971, JGA has grown to become a global leader in brand strategy and retail design. Named president in 1987 and chairman in 1995, Ken Nisch works internationally, with responsibilities that include client liaison and project strategy. Nisch was presented with the 2010 Retail Leadership Award at the Asia Retail Congress in Mumbai, India. In 2009, he was inducted into the Retail Design Institute Legion of Honor, recognizing his outstanding career achievement in the field of retail store design.

Q: Could you comment on how retailers are creating shopper experiences?

A: *The strategy of creating a whole environment in-store, with kiosks and big-screen TVs, has been abandoned in favor of creating shopper experiences that enrich the personal mobile device, both in and out of the store environment. The reason is that in the face of mobile shopper technology like iPads and smartphones, most retailers believe that they can't win "the device battle."*

Using devices as a part of a shopping experience has a few ramifications. First, devices accelerate the speed to purchase. Once researched, a purchase isn't bound by space or time. However, the seamless experience between digital and brick-and-mortar shopping can become so enjoyable that it can lead to delayed purchasing. The consideration phase of buying can be so enhanced that it becomes like FarmVille for Shoppers. It is the voyeuristic pleasure of shopping without the pain of purchasing.

The digital in-store experience is a fertile area of opportunity for retailers, who want to engage shoppers and close the deal. If you don't provide a compelling digital experience in-store, shoppers will use the device against you. In some cases, shoppers are using the retailer as a showroom for a purchase they intend to make online. In other cases, shoppers are looking at an item and decide to price-surf or do research on the spot, resulting in a sale for a competitor.

Here's a real-world example. Recently, my colleague was shopping for a mattress with her husband. They were having trouble deciding which mattress to buy, so they concluded that they needed to do more research. The sales associate, anxious to close the deal, offered to let them use his laptop to research the product. Here's what they found: lots of negative reviews! Naturally, they left the store without making a purchase.

Now, the retailer could have helped its sales associate by providing positive digital content to engage the shoppers. While this might not have been sufficient to overcome the negative reviews in this particular case, offering information and perspectives from the seller's view can help balance brand messaging. Sears is an example of a retailer that does a good job of consolidating shopper reviews, manufacturer information, and product and price comparison tools.

Q: Please discuss barriers to purchase and how retailers can overcome them.

A: *Shoppers have very few barriers to purchase today. They have access to goods, convenience in shopping, and knowledge of benefits, prices, and brands. But there is one thing they don't have: liquidity. They don't have money!*

Recently, the Wall Street Journal *ran an article about the financial fragility of Americans.*[21] *Half couldn't come up with $2,000 within a month.*

Buyers want liquidity, and sellers want them to have it. Retailers are making shoppers "co-conspirators" in the selling process now by giving them incentives to sell to their friends. These retailers are saying, "You and I are on the same side of the table. If you sell them something, we'll reward you. And, we won't tell your friends." This way, liquidity can be earned with shopper behavior, as you are saying in The Shopper Economy.

Other sellers are adding incremental value to sales, such as giving away complementary-category goods. Experience-based and entertain-

ment goods, like music downloads and televisions, work especially well as incremental value. For instance, one furniture seller was "giving away" a free television for every room full of furniture. This didn't compromise his brand or prices, yet it offered incremental value to the buyer. The sale was taken away from the electronics shop down the street.

Liquidity can also be released from the goods consumers already own. Wealthy divorcees are having champagne divorce sales in high-end hotels, like the Mondrian in LA. Some of the proceeds of these sales go to charity, some go to the organizer, and some go to the seller (former owner). While the champagne divorce sales involve high-end designer goods, a "rolling cycle of ownership" can squeeze incremental value out of ordinary goods, too.

In India, plastic bags are greener than paper. The reason is that they last 17 uses. India has a culture of a rolling cycle of ownership. Things start as premium use and go down. Only in a disposable culture is a paper bag greener. Rolling ownership recognizes the value in each use.

Retailers and brands that control the ownership cycle can restrict and expand the market. A brand can keep you as a brand loyalist by flanking the range of offerings with both new and preowned product. This is one way in which brands can extend a long-term relationship with the buyer, rather than having a one-off purchase.

Brands need to build relationships with shoppers through experiences. This was the first year that Wii and Sega had a down year. The reason is that a Wii game can cost upwards of $60, while an app costs two bucks. Apps are also used as rewards for behavior and are seen as "free" by shoppers.

The app is strategic for the retailer because it lowers the threshold to trial, removing a barrier to purchase. It also pushes shoppers into future purchase behavior. Rewarding shoppers with apps is looking at the lifetime value of the relationship, not a one-off sale.

CHAPTER 8 Recap: *Product as Souvenir*

- Earning points through various activities feels like getting something for "free." Most shoppers don't consciously recognize their time and effort as being equivalent to money.
- Many shoppers are ready to work for the rewards themselves, which would be beyond their ability or willingness to pay for with cash.
  - Labor-for-scrip programs are especially attractive during times of economic hardship and among people whose earning power is impeded.
  - Rewards can include big-ticket items like a college education or adding to a savings account, as well as fun indulgences like a vacation.
- Another impetus to labor is that the work feels like fun, not toil. This includes the gamification of shopper currency.
  - In a broad sense, making shopper tasks entertaining, competitive, or informative also opens a door to branded experiences.
- As shoppers become the new media channel, the product becomes the souvenir of their experience, and the experience is branding.
- Experience design is an emerging discipline and an important one for marketers to learn about. In the digital age, there will be more opportunities to create, manage, and brand shopper experiences—especially as more of these experiences are do-it-yourself mobile promotions.
  - There are methods for designing experiences, including Shedroff's six dimensions of experience.
  - Several companies have assigned a chief experience officer to focus on the customer experience, aligning all of

the functions of the firm to result in a unique and meaningful experience for the shopper and consumer.

*The digital in-store experience is a fertile area of opportu-
nity for retailers, who want to engage shoppers and close
the deal. If you don't provide a compelling digital experience in-store, shoppers will use the device against you.*

*A rolling cycle of ownership recognizes the value in each
use. Retailers and brands that control the ownership
cycle can restrict and expand the market.*

—Ken Nisch, Chairman, JGA

Loyalty

A person who deserves my loyalty receives it.

—Joyce Maynard, writer (1953–)

THE VALUE OF LOYALTY

In terms of valuing loyalty as a shopper currency, it is easier to start with what it isn't. It isn't advocacy (that's valuable, but it's a separate behavior); it isn't "satisfaction" or any score describing satisfaction; it isn't the "brand used most often" (BUMO) or favorite brand; it isn't brand evangelism (again, that's valuable, but it's not part of this discussion). In terms of shopper currency, loyalty is a commitment to buy a brand or product in the future. It's the promise of a future purchase, and in this sense it is the probability of a future stream of revenue.

Loyalty is about a commitment to buy. All managers want more sales, but these sales can have a few different origins. A shopper who buys only an average amount of a category could be persuaded to commit to giving the brand 100 percent of her requirements, or share of wallet. This is persuading a switcher to become loyal to one brand, without necessarily increasing her expenditures for the category. That shopper may never exceed the average consumption for that category, but the brand would benefit nonetheless.

> It is seven times cheaper to retain existing customers than to acquire new ones, according to the National Association of Retail Marketing Services.[1]
>
> Retention costs may be cheaper than acquisition costs, but the expenditure still needs to be less than the customer lifetime value (CLV). Programs must still be a profitable enterprise for the seller.

Another shopper may be persuaded to become a much heavier user of the category. For the heavy user, his 60 percent share of wallet may significantly outbuy the first shopper's 100 percent. This usage increase could stem from increases in the frequency of purchases or an increase in the depth of assortment of purchases (from upselling and cross-selling efforts, for example).

The question in the previous chapter was how to provide incentives for loyalty behaviors strategically. Brands must entice shoppers to join and participate, including offering attractive effort-reward ratios, no-brainer earning and redemption procedures, worthwhile rewards, and airtight security.

Pros and Cons of Running Points Programs

Loyalty programs can be strategically worthwhile in and of themselves if the retailer gathers and uses customer data effectively. However, this exchange must be financially attractive for the brand as well, and making loyalty programs profitable isn't as easy as it may appear. McKinsey wrote a wonderfully sensible white paper on this subject, "The Price of Loyalty." While this paper was published in 2000, it is still solidly relevant today. First, the authors pointed out that shoppers participating in loyalty programs aren't necessarily more loyal. The McKinsey article examined casual apparel and grocery loyalty programs. Yet, according to the article, "79 percent of customers in casual apparel and 70 percent in grocery say they are always seeking alternatives to their current retailers—percentages that far exceed the percentage of customers actively seeking alternatives in other categories."[2]

Second, the authors pointed out that loyalty programs don't necessarily increase spending. An example of an increase in spending could be a shopper who was upsold to buy more kinds of products from the retailer. While this may be the goal, it doesn't always happen. "Take a retailer providing a 2 percent rebate to program members. At variable

According to the 2011 Colloquy Loyalty Census, *"the average household holds 18 loyalty program memberships. Today, there are over two billion memberships in the U.S., up 16 percent from 1.8 billion in 2008."*[3]

margins of 30 percent . . . if only half of the members spent more money, that average spending increase would have to [be] 12 percent."[4] An increase of this magnitude is rare. In both the grocery and casual apparel areas, less than half of those enrolled in loyalty programs spent more.

To make matters worse for the seller, the basic costs of operating loyalty programs are high. This puts a tax on the rewards. But more than this, loyal participants in the program are further burdened by freeloaders, who get the benefits of the program without paying in.

Next, companies in the travel and credit industries have elevated the standards for rewards. Hotel chains, airlines, and credit card companies have higher economies of scale, so the incremental cost of rewarding one customer is insignificant to the seller, but very worthwhile for the buyer. This means that other kinds of businesses, particularly those with lower margins or smaller economies of scale, have trouble offering rewards that seem worth the shopper's time and effort. "A survey of consumers by Capital One Financial found that 57 percent of consumers had not redeemed points in the past three months. According to a *Dow Jones Newswires* report, 'Cardholders often cited the difficulty of redeeming the rewards, a lack of flexibility or a dearth of attractive redemption options.'"[5]

There are a few ways for companies to surmount these difficulties. First, sellers who may have a hard time offering worthwhile rewards can become part of a larger reward platform. A great case in point here is Sainsbury's in the United Kingdom. This grocer was losing ground to Tesco and had a tepid rewards points program. In 2003, Sainsbury's scrapped its own rewards system in favor of a coalition program called Nectar. Nectar allowed points to be collected and redeemed from multiple retailers, including BP, eBay, Amazon, the Gap, and Expedia.co.uk, to name a few. Within a few short years, Sainsbury's was issuing about half of the total points earned on Nectar and capturing more than half of those redeemed. Offering other rewards and ways to earn points enhanced the juiciness of Nectar for participants. Also, redemption of rewards fosters program participation and purchasing.

Another strategy is offering rewards with greater perceived value. In this case, the perceived value of the reward is greater than the actual, hard price of the reward. The shopper is getting some other utility out of the compensation. There have been several cases in which gasoline credits drove a significantly higher redemption rate than cash rewards of a *higher* value. This is because shoppers perceive that the gas credits are "worth" more. Similar to this example is offering value that is not strictly financial, such as fun, social status, or information. When foursquare offers a mayorship for checking into a venue most often, the badge itself isn't worth much in terms of cash. However, shoppers are ready to work for these badges. This kind of compensation can drive loyalty and participation programs too.

Many retailers may find it impossible to allow shoppers to earn their way to a week in the Caribbean (I don't mean a sweepstakes, but real earning). Beyond offering soft rewards (like mayorships), retailers can pique shoppers' interest in a loyalty program that offers frequent, if smaller, compensations. One example of this is CVS ExtraCare Rewards. The CVS rewards program offers 2 percent back with every purchase in-store and online, as well as an ExtraBuck for every two prescriptions. ExtraBucks are branded scrip that can be spent at CVS, at the shopper's discretion.

The CVS loyalty points can also be used to accrue to a college savings account called UPromise. UPromise is a coalition program. It is a multibrand, multiretailer platform that allows shoppers to accumulate points toward education. This is a very worthwhile reward for families that are trying to save for college. The loyalty program is tied to something much larger that the shopper is working toward, and hence becomes worth the shopper's effort. Working toward a larger, worthwhile reward in the midst of hard times is the same dynamic that was at work when S&H Green Stamps were popular.

Finally, companies can make loyalty programs work using Ken Nisch's concept of "a rolling cycle of ownership," described in the last chapter. This buyback program is a boon for retailers and shoppers. According to Ken,

> We are in a 'used' versus 'owned' culture, where something is of use to us for a while. Even though we are done with it, doesn't mean that it isn't of value to somebody else. We will see retailers trying to get a handle on the full cycle of a product, not just the first cycle.

Some day you can imagine that Tiffany, for example, could say, we'll buy back anything you bought from us. As long as you take the proceeds from that old product, and buy the new product from us. They will manage the buy-sell, resell process.

[For] companies that have issues in grey goods and counterfeiting, this is something that will help them protect their brand image.[6]

Nisch's phrase "rolling ownership" is similar to Best Buy's Buy Back policy, where shoppers can return obsolescent merchandise and buy the latest and greatest, as long as they buy it at Best Buy. While car dealerships have been using this model for years, retailers of smaller-ticket items can benefit from this model when shoppers are strapped for cash.

The retailer GameStop also offers its PowerUp reward points to gamers who are buying new or used games or returning used games to the store. While this loyalty may not seem like a big deal, the participation is staggering. Jen McMillan, vice president of loyalty and CRM for GameStop, shared at a conference in June 2011 that after only the first year, "67% of GameStop's 10 million members have enrolled at the 'Pro' level, paying a $14.99 annual membership fee for enhanced benefits. . . . Nearly 50% of GameStop's sales are now attached to a PowerUp club membership with the average member spending three times more than non-members."[7] Shoppers who pay to become members are much more committed than those who opt for the free version of the program. The percentage of people who pay to join is another measure of the success of the program.

Loyalty programs have been around for a long time. There are several firms and experts who have traveled up the learning curve and have much insight to share. To dig deeper into what motivates shoppers to commit to these programs, as well as what makes them profitable for companies, I interviewed three leading experts.

LOYALTY ROUNDTABLE

Phil Rubin, CEO and president, rDialogue
Bill Hanifin, managing director, Hanifin Loyalty LLC
Dan Frechtling, vice president, DS-IQ

Q: What makes a loyalty program an enticing business proposition?

PHIL: *First, you want to identify customers. As a retailer, you have people coming in the door who are making anonymous transactions. Anonymous transactions represent lost future sales. The loyalty proposition is, "If you make it worthwhile for me, I'll make it worthwhile for you." This is the quid pro quo of loyalty. This is a virtuous circle in that both parties keep winning. If you move away from that model, it doesn't work. An incentive built around breakage (i.e., the merchant's hoping that the customer doesn't redeem for the reward) is a terrible model.*

Second, you want to yield insights about your customers, which requires identifying your buyers. All of a sudden, you're smarter about your customers; you can recognize them for participation. You can ask them to do things. You have their attention!

Third, if you use the data well, you can grow your customers and keep them. No matter how you measure engagement, loyal customers are more profitable. Loyal customers give a business a 20 to 30 percent uplift on any given promotion, versus regular customers. Loyalty programs allow you to serve them better. This has implications for operations and for other decision-support situations, too. Loyalty programs have enterprise benefits.

Finally, you can measure results with a high degree of precision with a loyalty program. You don't get that from general advertising—or even from most online advertising. Loyalty programs offer a great path to greater organic growth.

BILL: *In this highly competitive world, there is only one price leader per category. If you aren't that brand, you need to find another strategy. Followers chasing the leader on price end up eroding customer service. This is where loyalty programs can come in and help differentiate a brand.*

The best loyalty programs offer continuous connection and sharing with the buyer, in a way that other marketing efforts, such as general advertising, sponsorships, and promotions, can't touch. These other approaches apply discounts at different points in time, whereas loyalty is ongoing and two-way.

DAN: *A loyalty program is enticing when it encourages heavy category buyers to convert into heavy brand buyers, without subsidizing existing heavy brand buyers.*

Q: Sometimes loyalty programs are expensive, unstoppable, and not always clearly profitable. Can you share the kinds of financial goals that work? How should companies value loyalty (programs)?

PHIL: *Loyalty should be profitable. If it isn't—it isn't a good idea. That's been documented by Bain and McKinsey. Where loyalty becomes expensive is when it doesn't have brand distinction or it is a me-too program. It must be aligned with the brand strategy. When loyalty isn't properly designed or executed, it doesn't work, and that's when it gets expensive!*

BILL: *Shoppers have the same complaint: "There are too many cards in my wallet!" You have to shift shoppers' attention to something they want, to a customer benefit. Customer strategies and good loyalty programs create a predisposition to buy your brand.*

How do companies achieve this? By creating enterprise-level, holistic solutions that put the customer at the center of their business. The programs that become margin eroders are those that are invented in someone else's boardroom. I mean that programs that chase a competitor's rewards program are poorly constructed. Someone at the top is saying, "Let's put a Twitter and Facebook presence out there. Our competitors have this." This is not a leadership mindset. The customer must be at the center of the strategy. This means understanding the customer's alternatives to your product, how customers like to communicate, and what they want.

Brands need to offer value to the customer all along the value chain. For example, a loyalty program means something different to a brand advocate from what it does to a fence-sitter. These customers need to be reached differently. Without a holistic, customer-centric strategy, a loyalty program is simply a deferred discount. This is why we've changed our language about what we deliver. Hanifin Loyalty delivers a holistic customer strategy for a company. A customer strategy is not always a loyalty program.

DAN: *Let me start with the last question. Companies should value loyalty based on its impact on lifetime value. But this is very hard to do with program execution. Results are mixed when programs try to manipulate individuals to behave in certain ways because individuals are at the same time trying to manipulate the system to extract the most value.*

I find it can be helpful to articulate the goal first and then find the company that works rather than vice versa. For example, to attract more people who are heavy consumers of your category (but not yet you) without subsidizing those who are already your heavy consumers, retailers do better than manufacturers.

Retailers:

1. *Have many products*
2. *Are capable of satisfying a range of shopper needs*
3. *By design have the data to drive decisions*

Manufacturers:

1. *Have fewer products*
2. *Are capable of satisfying fewer shopper needs*
3. *Have to work hard on research or spend money to acquire data to drive decisions*

Retailers can offer more choices to meet more needs. They can recommend categories that they know shoppers want but don't buy. For example, DS-IQ has found buyers of sandwich meat but not bread and helped retailers promote the latter. They can also spot changes in consumption, such as new births, and suggest items that shoppers need but are not aware of, such as products from the baby aisle. Finally, they can bundle disparate products into solutions, such as meat plus sauce plus buns plus charcoal equals BBQ. Manufacturers often settle for rewarding shoppers with more of what they have, which is more of the same, which naturally attracts those who are already loyal, yielding high subsidy cost.

Another way to end up in the same place (generate the highest lifetime value) is acting on an aggregate level through better intelligence about consumers. Unlike the mixed results of loyalty promotions, the data gathered from the loyalty infrastructure always adds value. Companies develop large databases of behavior that teach them how to identify the most valuable customers so that they can be recognized and retained. They also identify the least valuable, deal-seeking customers, whom they can choose to serve less to minimize losses.

Q: Can you share an example of a program that is a resounding success? One that is a dismal failure?

PHIL: *Amazon is a best-in-class example. The reason is that from the beginning it was committed to using its customer (loyalty) data in a smart, shopper-centric way. It integrated customer-specific data to communicate with customers during the preshop, shop, and postpur-chase phases. Amazon created a 360-degree customer experience.*

Sure, digital retail is easier than brick-and-mortar retailers in this way. Etail can identify the shopper and the purchase and the browsing history. But plenty of etailers don't use the data well.

The ultimate commitment is that I'll join Amazon Prime. Any-time you get someone to pay extra to do business with you, and make such a future commitment, it's an indication that the loyalty is work-ing. For the shopper, it is an economic opportunity cost of doing busi-ness elsewhere.

In the beginning of 2011, across the board, companies were saying that loyalty is the number one strategic priority. But there is a differ-ence between companies with loyalty programs and truly customer-centric companies, like Amazon. Bezos obsesses about what will make customers loyal, buy more, and have a good experience.

On the other hand, Blockbuster missed the digital channel. Net-flix built a model around it. Blockbuster was the channel for the movie you wanted to play at home; it did not add value as a channel. Netflix lets you rank the movies and then uses the data to recommend which ones you will like. Netflix saves you time and money, delivering what you want. But it's not a transactional model, like Blockbuster's. It's a relationship model.

When loyalty is done right, you step above the transaction and get to emotional loyalty. The first time a shopper buys, it is just a transac-tion, but not yet a relationship. Smart retailers are setting up a long-term relationship. It's like in the movie When Harry Met Sally, *"At least kiss me when you do that." . . . It takes time for romance.*

BILL: *In terms of failure, many private-label credit cards are offering the wrong proposition. A shopper, who may not be looking for another credit card, is offered an immediate 10 or 20 percent discount on the purchases at the cash register. The shopper may go for the discount and the card, which is issued instantly at the point of sale. What happens to the card? It goes in the drawer. It was a single-use discount. There are way too many of those.*

Of course, American Express Rewards is a very successful program. American Express developed its program and positioned it so that it's not just a payment card. It is creating experiences and access to privileges that go beyond payment. The OPEN Forum for small business is a great example. It has resources for the business owner. It's a clubby atmosphere; it's not about interest rates and annual fees. Small business owners want an Amex because it delivers so much more value.

Another great example of differentiation is U.S. Bank. U.S. Bank came up with its FlexPerks program after Northwest Airlines was bought by Delta. The bank had offered Northwest Airlines miles prior to the buyout. Most people like the airline miles perks. The free seat is great, but the travel experience is arduous and dismal. U.S. Bank distinguished itself from the other miles programs by kicking in an extra $25 with every earned trip. The $25 can be used for amenities, like extra legroom or checking baggage. This kind of benefit really speaks to customers; it feels like the bank understands what it's like to walk in my shoes.

DAN: *Given the challenges, it can be hard to execute loyalty programs that delight the manufacturer, retailer, and shopper. But it can be done.*

DS-IQ ran a campaign that persuaded shoppers loyal to a brand in the canned soup category to buy that brand in the frozen dinner category. While the redemption rate for the frozen item was 9 percent among all shoppers, it was nearly 50 percent for those who were already buying the brand as a canned soup. Furthermore, nearly all shoppers were new to the frozen category, which greatly pleased the retailer.

Timing is everything. Picture a loyal user of Gillette Mach 3. In other words, imagine a product with high loyalty and low switching. The problem for Gillette and the retailer may not be as much what he'll buy as it is when he'll buy. Research has shown that the fifth blade may be used as long as the first four combined, because the buyer forgets week after week to replenish.

This buyer won't respond to a Schick offer. He also won't respond to a Mach 3 offer after just buying a five-pack.

But when that fifth blade dulls, he may well respond to a new Gillette Fusion ProGlide upsell offer, because the brand and the timing are perfectly relevant.

Q: There are many opportunities for shoppers to link their points programs. Do you think the market may go toward a universal virtual currency? What are the pros and cons of that from a business perspective?

PHIL: *A universal scrip is unlikely in the United States. In the United States, collation programs haven't taken hold. You have some strong coalition programs in other (much smaller) countries such as Canada and in the United Kingdom and Australia. Here brands don't want to make themselves subservient to others or a group of others.*

In terms of virtual currency, American Express Membership Rewards points is the most valuable one we have. From a branded payments standpoint, it can kill everyone. Its heritage is built around using customer data well and linking to others—for both merchant partners and card carriers.

As a retailer, I'll pay a higher fee for Amex than for Visa, because it delivers a higher-value customer. Also, Amex helps its retailers succeed in the way Coke helps its fountain customers succeed. Amex knows it will get a disproportionate share when it helps the merchant and creates exclusive value for its cardmembers.

BILL: *Coalition programs come closest to this now. This is the preeminent model outside the United States. Examples include Dots in Brazil, Bonus in Peru, and Nectar in the United Kingdom.*

Well-defined groups of partners can also create a successful coalition. Esso in Canada has a partnership program with HBC, RBC, and Sears Canada. At the pump, consumers select which points program they want to earn credit in. The points are already linked.

In fact, the accumulated financial liability for these points programs is something that banks want companies to burn off. Partners can help with this. Tesco, the largest grocer in the United Kingdom, was a great example of this. Tesco's Clubcard was having a problem because its funding rate was transparent to the shopper. The perceived value of its points was quite low. The solution was to recruit partners to help burn off the financial liability and to help mask the funding rate. They gave more leverage to customers who redeemed at those partners. The rewards had greatly improved perceived value, and Tesco's financial liability was reduced.

Even so, I can't see a "white label" scrip right now; the reason is branding. Companies want to have control over the branding, the program, and the rewards. In Canada, for example, well over 60 percent of households have Air Miles accounts. So the company needs to justify the value of the program to its partners. Recently there have been a few defections from these programs.

DAN: *Points are attractive for several reasons. For the enterprise, they encourage purchases within one's own portfolio of products or services rather than yielding savings that are ultimately spent elsewhere. For the consumer, points can be made more "fun" through gamification or through challenges that persuade shoppers to spend more by spurring feelings of achievement and competition.*

But they are also unattractive. The enterprise faces the beat-them-or-join-them dilemma—commercial players resist supporting another company's currency because they prefer to be in the center. The consumer doesn't like the fact that points are restricted to the participating merchants, and therefore are a less valuable currency.

To address these barriers, it may take an 800-lb gorilla to compel others to fall in line. The gorilla may present a large enough business opportunity that merchants are better off joining than not joining. And consumers may find the currency freely traded enough to put up with the smaller points economy. Air Miles in Canada and the United Kingdom has established such a position.

Q: What's the vision for loyalty programs in the next five years? (Ten years?)

PHIL: *The lines between the customer experience and loyalty programs will (and should) become blurrier. Customer data will become more fully baked into the experience of buying and using, and those data, in turn, will be more fully utilized by the enterprise, not only for serving the customer, but also for making more customer-centric decisions.*

The biggest issue on the CMO's agenda is integration. Right now, strategies and results are siloed. There are several data streams: the website, social media, outbound traditional marketing, and in-store marketing. The data aren't synced up. For example, the foursquare people won't know I spent $40 at a particular venue unless (and this is a great example) I've linked my American Express card to my foursquare account.

BILL: *Loyalty programs for the last 30 years were largely built by boomers for boomers. The shift now is to the Consumer 2.0, who has the "always-on" lifestyle. We estimate that there are about 150 million people who live this way in the United States.*

These consumers aren't willing to wait two years to earn something they want. They want immediacy. They also want more liquidity in their rewards. Rewards will become more fungible. We can already see this emerging in the rise of Points.com. This web-based service is a currency exchange for miles and points, across multiple brands and programs. Consumers pay a small percentage of their total to consolidate their points into a single account of their choosing. Value can be donated or gifted. Another option is to roll all of the scrip into a PayPal account, which can be used immediately to purchase goods and services online.

This new consumer is different in another way too. Consumer 2.0 relies on his or her trusted network of friends before purchasing. The conversation in social media is creating a predisposition to buy or not buy, in the preshop. The implication is that marketers need to have more of an engagement philosophy than a strictly transactional philosophy.

Brands can reward shoppers for activities before an actual transaction takes place. Rewarding nontransaction behaviors, like getting educated about the brand or engaging with others about the brand, may become more of an established way to presell brands.

One danger is that this group has been heavily reenforced with the Groupon mentality. Right now they are looking for deep discounts, like 50 percent off. Just offering a 10 percent discount won't get their attention. There need to be other enticing reasons to engage.

DAN: *Technology enables loyalty programs to make it easier to buy, not just cheaper. Encouraging loyalty without bribery is the future. Interestingly, while conventional loyalty programs are in the province of marketing, future loyalty will be equal parts product and marketing.*

One example is Netflix's recommendation algorithm, which has evolved and improved over time to provide more fulfilling title suggestions. For example, the system has discovered that people rate movies differently depending on how long ago they saw them, what day of the week they were asked, and so on.

Another example is Starbucks Cards, which began as stored value and now have extended into mobile phones via the Starbucks Card mobile app. Adopting the card leads people to spend more. Users admit that flashing their phones for payment is fun and self-expressive. Google is trying something similar with Google Wallet.

Apple's common OS across devices—phones, music players, tablets, and more—creates its own loyalty via ease of use.

CHAPTER 9 Recap: *Loyalty*

- In terms of shopper currency, loyalty is a commitment to buy a brand in the future. It is the probability of a future purchase.
- A good loyalty program creates brand preference by creating an enterprise-level strategy that puts the customer at the center of the business.
- Retailers need to make anonymous transactions unattractive for the buyer. Engaging loyalty programs can eliminate anonymity and lead to insights about shoppers. Anonymous transactions represent lost future sales.
- Successful loyalty programs offer worthwhile rewards to shoppers, with easy redemption procedures. Brands need to keep the focus on the customer, while keeping an eye on profitability.
- Sellers that may have a hard time offering worthwhile rewards can become part of a coalition, a larger multibrand reward platform.
  - Even aligning with a few key partners can help a brand burn off the financial liability of carrying rewards on its books, as well as enhance the perceived value of rewards to its shoppers.
- Retailers of fast-moving goods can pique interest in a loyalty program by offering frequent, if smaller, compensations that are redeemable immediately.
- Shoppers who pay to become members are much more committed than those who opt for the free version of any points program. The percentage of people who pay to join is another measure of success of the program. GameStop PowerUp Rewards and Amazon Prime are good examples of this.

- In the future, reward value will become more fungible, more liquid, and more immediate.

- Consumers are consulting their network of friends and family about purchases in the preshop period, making social media critical in the consideration phase. So, rewarding nontransaction behaviors, like getting educated about the brand or engaging with others about the brand, may become more of an established way to presell brands among members-to-be.

10

Valuing Attention

WHAT'S IT WORTH?

What is attention worth? For many companies, the correlated question is more immediate: What is advertising worth? This topic is as old as advertising itself. While there have been numerous models showing the impact of above-the-line advertising on sales and goodwill, the ROI of promotions has been easier to measure directly. Attention itself is worth more today than it was in past decades, when there were fewer messages competing for mindshare. The price of delivering attention—or at least attention expressed as eyeballs, impressions, listeners, and pass-along readers—had been dictated by the supply of and demand for space on television, radio, print, and outdoor.

The relative worth of delivered messages is usually measured in terms of the impact on the brand. These measures include awareness, the evoked set (the consideration set), brand imagery, purchase intent (often a surrogate for likelihood of conversion), and cohort imagery, among others.

Today social and mobile media can influence the brand differently from traditional channels. Brand imagery has been part of marketing communications for decades. In the past, a shopper not only knew that Budweiser was a beer and might consider Budweiser when searching for beer, but also knew that it was the "King of Beers." There was cohort imagery as well. Who drank Budweiser? Advertising on television gave the viewer an idea of what Budweiser drinkers were like. Remember the "Whassup?!" ads? Those ads showed Budweiser drinkers as being a group of laid-back friends, in contrast to those who weren't in the brand franchise (nerds). Of course, beer drinkers could see who was drinking the beer in bars and restaurants and at parties, too. But today, at least part of the cohort definition is coming from trending social media and one's personal social graph. The media context of awareness building and attention reflects on the brand. To an extent, this has always been the case, but now, with Yelp reviews, wall postings, recommendations, star ratings, "trending now" alerts, LivingSocial-type deals, and "likes" or "+1's," the social context of brand building is more influential than ever. To some extent social media are advocacy, but social media also drive attention and awareness.

So brand presence has an emerging set of metrics, including keyword searches, ratings, reviews, number of shares and likes, among others. Nielsen BuzzMetrics analyzes content from millions of blogs, user groups, and social networks. This comprehensive monitor measures the scale and depth of brand buzz. There are other companies offering web buzz monitoring services as well.

THE NEW MODEL: SHOPPER ATTENTION AS CURRENCY

Brands are beginning to compensate the viewer directly. This is a new attention model in the digital age. The shopper agrees to exchange his time and attention for virtual currency or other compensation. Attention is currency in the shopper economy.

There are a few consumer-facing companies that use the attention-for-value paradigm as a business model, including Varolo and Bing. Varolo (http://www.varolo.com/) is a web-based channel for advertisers; it reaches a group of consumers who watch ads in exchange for money and prizes. Consumers who participate in Varolo earn chances to win a big raffle when they watch ads. If they recruit their friends to watch ads, too, then they have built a Varolo "village." Every time people in a particular village watch ads, the original recruiter gets an actual paycheck (not just a chance to win) commensurate with the number of viewers and the number of ads watched. In this case, the advertising budget has shifted directly to the viewer.

In another example, Bing offers reward points for using its search engine. Using a search engine is a form of attention; virtual currency gives surfers a reason for choosing Bing.

One of Bing's initial offerings shows the success that this approach can enjoy. Bing offered shoppers looking for dinner ideas the opportunity to click on a "Dining In" button or a "Dining Out" button. Rewards were offered for either choice.

There were 1.2 million engagements resulting from this offer. About 75 percent clicked through to the Bing Facebook Fan Page, and more than a third of responders shared the link. The aver-

> *"Now Facebook users can earn credits simply by participating with the advertiser to get free stuff," said CEO Jay Samit. "This kind of advertising satisfies what brands have been looking for—an opt-in experience with a reach greater than TV and highly targeted."[1]*

age time spent with the ad was nearly a minute and a half. This successful program was powered by a company called SocialVibe (http://www.socialvibe.com/).

> "SocialVibe . . . is no stranger to Facebook—they power the advertising in Zynga hits like CityVille, Mafia Wars and many others and reach 200 million gamers a month by offering ads from brands like Lexus, American Express and Pepsi."[2]

In order to get further insight into how this new advertising model is working, I spoke with SocialVibe's chief marketing officer, Larry Lieberman.

INTERVIEW WITH LARRY LIEBERMAN, CMO, SOCIALVIBE

Larry brings more than 25 years of experience in connecting major brands with emerging technologies, including his role as CMO for cloud-computing virtual animation studio Aniboom and CMO for Sir Richard Branson's Virgin Comics and Virgin Animation. He has also held senior marketing positions at Comedy Central, Warner Music Group, and MTV, where he built media brands and led sales teams with more than $1 billion in revenue from the United States and overseas.

Q: Please explain what makes SocialVibe special.

A: *SocialVibe is a leading engagement marketing solution that guarantees active consumer attention. The appeal of our platform is that the consumer has a stake in the sites that feature SocialVibe ad engagements. This reinforces the message that consumers have a stake in the brands they interact with.*

Today, consumers select which media they consume, and that includes advertising.

Advertising used to be a one-way monologue. It ignored the consumer's value, or the possibility that customers might want to respond to the company. Our platform recognizes both.

Q: What makes pay-for-performance advertising an enticing business proposition for companies?

A: *"Pay for performance" can have a derogatory connotation. SocialVibe doesn't pay a consumer for performance. Rather, we acknowledge that her time has value.*

The critical success factor for our advertising is that the consumer gets something when she chooses to look at the ad. The value exchange is in the language (and the currency) of the site where the consumer spends time—for example, points in the game the consumer is playing at that moment. The motivation is contextual, which makes it relevant to the consumer. The context drives the relevancy.

Direct marketers have known for a long time that consumer responsiveness goes up when the distance between the consumer's mindset and the product message is minimized.

This really is different from "pay for performance." We use the phrase "value exchange" to describe what occurs more accurately. Consumers are given value for agreeing to launch the brand experience; they don't get rewarded by how many minutes they spend. It is still incumbent on SocialVibe to create brand experiences that are so relevant and interesting that consumers want to stay until the end.

Q: What makes for a satisfying user experience?

A: *Consumers love the unexpected! It's a basic aspect of human nature. Give me something that surprises me or initiates curiosity—don't give* me what I expect. Consumers watch hockey for the fights, or auto races for the crashes. It's the anomaly that they are looking for.

There are four parts to a SocialVibe engagement:

1. *The first is the* launch. *Let's say the consumer is playing CityVille. In the context of the game, SocialVibe's offer is compelling enough to encourage consumers to click on the launch point and click through to the ad. The entire experience begins when users choose to launch the ad. This is not a pop-up. This is not a pre-roll. The value exchange is the first step. That is what compels consumers to "exchange" their active attention. A great brand experience takes them through steps 2 through 4.*

2. The brand experience *happens next, in the 750 × 500 window on the screen. The brand experience frequently includes video, polling, store locators, image uploads, and coupon downloads—all with high levels of attention and interactivity.*

3. *Next, the consumer takes* action *as a result of seeing that brand experience. This can involve clicking on the advertiser's site, downloading content, or responding to a call to action in any number of ways.*

4. *Finally,* consumers often share *the content with friends and family via Facebook and Twitter. This is earned media, and it exponentially expands the reach of our advertisers' message, even when consumers aren't given incentives.*

In terms of effectiveness, we usually see recall scores upwards of 94 percent correct on watched ads. That is incredibly effective messaging.

Q: How is SocialVibe different from a Varolo-type model (e.g., paying U.S. dollars for viewers to watch back-to-back ads)?

A: *When you reward people in U.S. dollars, there is no contextual relevance to connect the user to the brand experience. U.S. dollars certainly have value, but they are generic, without any personality.*

It's like the guy who donates blood for a buck. He doesn't really care about saving a life; he cares about the buck. The people in a paid audience for an ad can be similar. They don't really care about the ad; they care about the buck.

Brands want to hit the right audience. For example, every time a cat litter ad is seen by someone who doesn't own a cat, the brand is wasting money. You want to hit the right audience. Now, buying ads on cute cat sites may deliver better than your average site for hitting cat owners, but it still isn't a guarantee.

How do you find the right user—in this case, only cat owners? I ask them! When the user clicks onto the engagement, he is asked a question: "Do you own a cat?" If the answer is yes, he gets a cat litter ad. Non-cat owners get a different ad. The user self-selects the relevant ad based on a simple, noninvasive question.

The age of transparency fights with the age of tracking. Marketers can't have it both ways.

Behavioral targeting claims that it is 60 percent accurate. Why not just ask consumers if they own a cat, for example, and have them self-select? This is our technique. True Targeting™ delivers the right ad to the right consumer at the right time. We've discovered that 98 percent of the people answered accurately when we validated the True Targeting technique.

SocialVibe Average Performance Metrics

- 100 percent consumer-initiated ads
- 80 percent completion rate
- 63 seconds average time spent per user
- 41 percent visit a fan page or website
- 10 to 40 percent share the ads[3]

When is the right time? When the consumer is willing to engage. It's when the consumer decides, "I'll watch this ad now." That's the right time. The right ad is a compelling engagement experience; it's enlightening, entertaining, and surprising.

In terms of the value exchange, virtual currency makes better use of emotional response and behaviors than real dollars do. A person who is immersed in a virtual experience, like Pandora or games, places an artificially high value on the virtual currency related to that experience.

To date, SocialVibe is just passing the 50 million engagement mark. We have engaged so many consumers so many times now that we can provide consumers with an experience that they want and the advertiser with a relevant audience that is paying attention.

Q: What is your vision for advertising and marketing in the next five years?

A: *I see less change than most of the futurists. I think that communications innovations are anchored in devices and environments—and the proliferation of portable devices is what is driving that change. Most advertising has done a good job—not perfect, but a consistently good job—of evolving and understanding why consumers like brands and buy products.*

The biggest change will be improvements in the effectiveness and relevance of mobile and tablet ads. Right now, they are generally intrusive or irrelevant. In just a few years, I've seen great strides in terms of relevance and dialogue. One of my favorite campaigns is the Pepsi Refresh program, which makes great use of two-way media.

Q: Do you think that a service like Klout could change the value exchange for consumers and marketers?

A: *Yes, it could. But as a practical matter, it doesn't change my world. For example, this morning on the* Today Show, *there was a story about a guy from Cincinnati with a very high Klout score. He was an avowed steak lover and a loyal customer of one particular chain of steak houses. During a flight to New York, he tweeted about how much he'd love a steak when he got to New York City. Sure enough, when he landed at Newark Airport, Morton's was there to greet him with a porterhouse to go. Bless this guy, his Klout score validates his celebrity status, and now he's a media property. At the end of the day, should anyone care? Probably not.*

At SocialVibe, we want to talk to everyone who is likely to buy our clients' products—not just folks with high Klout scores.

Q: Do you think we will see a universal virtual currency?

A: *No, I don't think we will. For games and hobbies, contextual relevance overrides global efficiencies. Look at the drachma and the lira—they were replaced by the euro to assist bankers and facilitate cross-cultural transactions, not because the typical Greek or Italian wanted to let them go. Most gamers have the same local-focused mindset. They are not concerned about transferring their currency between sites, and they pride themselves on the value of their earnings within their favorite games. For advertisers, there is the added benefit of using in-game credits to speak to consumers in the context of their favorite environments; removing the local context reduces the perceived value of the reward. I can't see it.*

CASE STUDIES

Giving people incentives to opt into an advertisement, pay attention and participate where necessary, and share the advertisement with friends are the goals of interactive ads. Here are a few case studies showing how these ads work and the results.

GE Ecomagination Campaign: "Tag Your Green"

GE launched an interactive advertisement for the Ecomagination campaign called "Tag Your Green" (see Figure 10.1). The campaign was developed in partnership with BBDO, SocialVibe, and Speedshape.

The interactive ad enabled people to submit photos of wind, light, or water in order to raise money for charities that use alternative energy solutions. The goal of the campaign was to get people to not only think about the environment, but also translate participation into real impact for the charities by counting each photo upload as a microdonation. Users across SocialVibe's network of web properties, such as Zynga's social games, Causes.com, Pan-

| Figure 10.1 | GE's "Tag Your Green" Campaign |

Source: SocialVibe

dora, and IMVU, were able to complete the photo donation task all within SocialVibe's rich media ad unit.

The campaign at once sparked social interaction through photo tagging, uploads, and sharing. It also translated into real donations to Practical Action (wind), charity: water (water), and the d.light design's Oecusse (East Timor) Project (light). People spent an average of 150.5 seconds interacting with the GE content, and they uploaded tens of thousands of photos to the "Tag Your Green" photo galleries. The campaign also saw a 69 percent click-through rate on Facebook shares.

Demo link: http://www.svnetwork.com/activities/594.

Additional information: http://mashable.com/2010/10/21/ ge-tag-your-green/.

Kia Motors America Campaign: "Big Game Tournament"

Kia partnered with SocialVibe to introduce the all-new Optima to social gamers. Kia positioned Optima as the exclusive automotive sponsor of Zynga's "Big Game Tournament" for players across FarmVille, PetVille, Mafia Wars, and Café World. Players were able to earn free game currency by participating in a virtual football game sponsored by the 2011 Optima. Throughout game play, players were treated with interactive Kia Optima content as well as the opportunity to share the engagement with their friends through Facebook or Twitter.

Zynga's Big Game Tournament, powered by SocialVibe and sponsored by Kia, allowed millions of social media users to immerse themselves in their own "Big Game" and connect with the brands in a highly social and relevant way (Figure 10.2). The integration allowed Kia to reach consumers beyond its Super Bowl television spot and engage with them in a meaningful way online.

| Figure 10.2 | Zynga's Big Game Tournament |

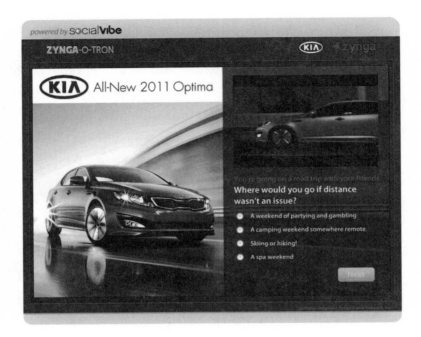

Kia's virtual football game engagement yielded Social-Vibe's highest ever average time spent per user, with people spending an average of 170 seconds interacting with the content.

Demo link: http://www.svnetwork.com/activities/672.

CHAPTER 10 Recap: *Valuing Attention*

- In the past, the price of delivering attention—or at least attention expressed as eyeballs, impressions, listeners, and pass-along readers—was largely dictated by the supply of and demand for space on television, radio, print, and outdoor.
- Today, attention is also garnered on the web through sharing, social sites, user-generated content, and more.
  - There are several companies that measure "brand buzz," including Radian6, Nielsen, Meltwater Buzz, and others.
- An emerging media model is compensating the viewer directly for her attention. The shopper agrees to exchange her attention for virtual currency or some other reward. Attention is currency in the shopper economy.
  - There are a few companies that use the attention-for-value paradigm as a business model, including Varolo, Facebook, and SocialVibe.
- SocialVibe uses the phrase "value exchange." Consumers are given value in exchange for agreeing to the brand experience.
- In terms of the value exchange, in-game currency often makes better use of emotional response and behaviors than real dollars do.
  - In-game currency is valued very highly by the person who is immersed in the virtual experience. The user places more value on that currency because of context than the currency is strictly worth on an exchange-rate basis.

11

Marketing Implications for the Near Term

TEN IMPLICATIONS FOR MARKETERS

So far, we've explored several aspects of value exchange in the shopper economy and interviewed experts in the field. This chapter suggests marketing implications for the near term. Some of the implications arise from key learning, while others result from changing market conditions.

1. Enabled by Technology, Shopper Behaviors Are Becoming a Form of Currency That Can Be Exchanged for Other Forms of Value

Marketing is morphing into a deliberate and intimate relationship between the brand and the shopper. Shoppers are remunerated for behaviors that add worth to the brand's value chain. In exchange for advocating or participating in auto-promotions, shoppers are rewarded with virtual currencies. These aren't frequent shopper programs, and this is not a "buy to get" scheme. However, the participants are compensated immediately and personally.

To the extent that this value can be banked and redeemed at will, and to the extent that it is acknowledged as payment, it acts as "real" currency for buyers. This currency will become a more important force in the market as the number of outlets for redemption expands. Today this means larger coalitions of retailers and brands accepting a common form of scrip or setting up exchange rates. In fact, websites like Points.com already allow nearly any type of digital scrip to be deposited into a PayPal account, from which buyers can acquire a vast range of goods and services.

Another factor accelerating the acceptance and use of digital scrip will be an increase in self-serve points of sale that can accept scrip as payment or partial payment for a purchase. This is already a feature at these points of sale: Esso pay-at-the-pump stations, Target stores that accept Shopkick's mobile bar code for redemption, and Amazon's online checkout (using linked accounts from American Express or Visa), among others. Establishing frictionless payment methods helps to increase the use of virtual currencies because the exchange is instant at the point of purchase. In addition, most consumers think of virtual currency as "not real money," and this will encourage increased redemption of this value in an era of prolonged unemployment or recession.

Not all shopper behaviors are equally valuable to marketers. I am suggesting that there are four rudimentary buckets of shopper currency: attention, participation, advocacy, and loyalty. These behaviors are generally escalating in value; however, as each brand has a different audience and objectives to meet, they may be valued differently on a business-by-business basis.

2. Shoppers Are the Medium

Each shopper is a media vehicle, able to reach and possibly influence hundreds or thousands of other shoppers. As each person's social graph becomes ubiquitous within digital contexts and accessible throughout the shopping cycle, the ability to harness the power of shopper labor will become critical to a brand's success. The implication is that shoppers are assuming the labor of brand communications. We will see more pass-along promotions and "do-it-yourself" advocacy programs that reward shopper-generated endorsements with virtual currency and deferred discounts.

In addition, there will be more auto-promotions, in which shoppers are recording their own behavior in selling to themselves. In this kind of self-serve promotion, shoppers are assuming the labor of promoting the brand to *themselves*, in exchange for virtual currency and soft currency. In many cases, the sales associate will be completely disintermediated. The marketing labor and budget have shifted directly onto the shopper.

Finally, in the shopper economy, each shopper is a brand. The shopper-advocate who is relied upon by other shoppers for information is himself a filter. Using movie reviews is a good example. I know that my friend Ted has very different tastes in movies from what I do. Whenever he likes a comedy, I am sure to hate it. Or if my Aunt Lisa likes a fashion designer, I know I should check him out too, since I admire her style. These are simple ways in which shoppers are brands and filters.

The shopper-as-brand model colors the message to the recipient. However, it also compels the advocate to screen or modify brand messages based on her persona. The more cultivated the social media persona, the more stringent the filter on brand endorsements. This takes us to our next implication.

3. The Age of the Personal Endorsement Deal Is upon Us

Shoppers know that their word is valuable. Klout scores are an attempt to quantify the individual's level of influence in the digital realm. Buddy Media and other similar firms are able to track the sharing, resharing, and purchasing patterns of endorsers and their followers. With ranking tools and tracking mechanisms like these at our fingertips, marketers will soon be recruiting paid advocates from among the ranks of ordinary consumers. (Some marketers already are.)

Of course, to a certain extent, this is nothing new. From Tupperware party hostesses to nightclubbers wearing temporary tattoos, consumers have been striking bargains with brands for decades. However, the tracking and the scale are new. Shoppers are generating content that is broadcast on the web, extending each person's reach and scale of advocacy. Furthermore, brands can track both the audience reached and the extent to which a particular consumer influenced the purchasing behavior of other consumers. This means that the financial value of each brand proponent can be calculated, and the reward to that person can be determined within the context of the brand's profitability. This brings us back to the idea of the labor market for shopper behavior. In a sense, the committed endorser is an employee of the company; there may be a fine-print contract to this effect, too. No longer is the role of endorser limited to celebrities alone. The age of the "everyman" celebrity endorser is here.

4. Advocates Are Not Necessarily the Same as Heavy Buyers; Each Should Be Marketed to Differently

Interestingly, both the *Harvard Business Review* article, "How Valuable Is Word of Mouth?" and the interview with Keith Simmons reported the same phenomenon: that the best brand advocates are not necessarily the same as heavy buyers. These can be (and often are) two very different groups of people.

There are a few big implications of this. The first is that marketers can't assume that their most loyal customers are their best advocates. This needs to be tested on a brand-by-brand basis. If these are indeed different shopper segments, they should be marketed to differently. Advocates should be given better tools for spreading the word and recruiting more users and recruiters. Rewards can be determined using the incremental revenue streams from advocates' efforts. On the other hand, loyalists should be upsold and cross-sold. DIY promotions or self-promotions can be the digital mechanisms of choice for heavy users, even if those programs are masked with gamification.

Moving forward, marketers might find it useful to divide their shoppers into the heavy-user group and the heavy-advocate group. These two audiences need to be given different incentives because they are motivated by different stimuli. Incentives for advocacy may differ dramatically from incentives for usage. The barriers to shopper advocacy are not the same as the barriers to purchase. This difference may give rise to different shopper marketing paradigms from those that are currently in circulation.

5. Virtual Currency Will Be Increasingly Frictionless and Fungible with Fiat Currencies

According to consumer loyalty expert Bill Hanifin, "Consumers aren't willing to wait two years to earn a reward. They want immediacy. They also want more liquidity in their rewards. Rewards will become more fungible." And the environment is ripe to meet these demands. Mobile technology, gamification, and the increased pervasiveness of virtual currencies will usher in an age of frictionless digital currencies that will have immediate liquidity, ubiquity, and fungibility in terms of their exchange with traditional fiat currencies.

As a case in point, Esso in Canada offers a reward system that allows consumers to choose, right at the pump, whether to pay in cash or points. The same mechanism is at work in the purchase of airline tickets—consumers can pay all or part of their fare with credit card points or frequent flyer miles. While these examples may not seem revolutionary, they do point to a change in how consumers can choose to pay, at the point of sale.

While loyalty points programs like Esso's may be seen as "deferred discount" programs, increasingly shoppers will have the option to participate in a value-exchange program that does not require purchase. This earned value will be convertible to liquid assets at self-checkout registers everywhere. If the global economy worsens, or if pressure on prices worsens, consumers may look to earn and spend this alternative currency more and more.

6. Brands That Recognize the Financial Value in Preowned Goods Will Expand Their Customer Base and Will Command More Customer Loyalty than Those That Do Not

Savvy brands will own both primary and secondary markets for their goods; that is, they will own the whole product life cycle, including reuse, and will provide incentives for buyback programs. In turn, shoppers will have a lot of choices to consider when making a purchase, especially a higher-ticket purchase. Shoppers will be committing to a relationship with the seller, in which the retailer is the buyer in the aftermarket for the product.

A recent example was Best Buy's Buy Back Program. Best Buy agreed to give the shopper some recompense for outdated technology that was purchased at Best Buy. This program was reviewed in the February 10, 2011, issue of *Consumer Reports*. The author, James Wilcox, concluded that the "issue is whether the prepaid buy back concept is a worthwhile one. For most of us, I don't think it is. For one, you're prepaying for a service you might never use. For another, unless you plan to buy a new TV every six months, the amount you'll receive isn't likely to be meaningful. For example, if you keep your TV for two years, in the best-case scenario you'll only get up to 10 percent of the original purchase price, and after four years you'd get nothing."[1]

The problem with the Best Buy Program, from the shopper's perspective, is the cost. If the cost of the program were lower, or if it were even free, then Best Buy would retain more loyal users. However, the cost to the retailer would be higher, of course. This cost would have to be considered using calculations of the lifetime value of the customer, possibly based on purchase history. Is the lifetime value of the customer worth it? Perhaps an algorithm, based on purchasing history and other factors, could be developed that could discern which customers would be eligible for which levels of buyback discounts.

A few months after the Buy Back Program was introduced and panned, Best Buy announced a 30 percent drop in profits. Some analysts cited eBay and Amazon as fierce competition for the brick-and-mortar model. However, at this point, shoppers are still game at least look at product in a physical store. I believe that if Best Buy were to take the lifetime value of its customers seriously by offering them a real Buy Back Program, the firm could reinvigorate its business model while committing customers to future purchases. This program could help prevent customers from using the retailer as a showroom for Internet purchases.

Retailers who see the lifetime value of customers as key to the long-term health of their businesses will benefit from allowing their customers to release liquidity from the assets they purchased at the franchise. If financing becomes harder for the average consumer to attain, then lifetime value programs will increase in importance.

7. Experience Design Will Become Very Important for Branding, as Shoppers Will Encounter Retailers and Brands Everywhere, All the Time

As the labor market for shopper behavior expands, experience design (XD) will become an increasingly sophisticated discipline for marketers. While shoppers are working to earn value, their labor becomes part of the branding experience. Therefore, XD must be at the forefront of branding.

"Experience design (XD) is the practice of designing products, processes, services, events, and environments with a focus placed on the quality of the user experience and culturally relevant solutions."[2] I like the emphasis here on "culturally relevant solutions" because it points to the context of the experience as an important component of the solution. The context can be within a game, like FarmVille or SCVNGR, or it can be within one's personal social graph.

Nathan Shedroff, the author of *Making Meaning*, describes six dimensions of experience that are useful for designing meaningful experiences. Thinking in these terms is pertinent for marketers, who have the task of engaging masses of people who are participating in brand activities every day.

Furthermore, many engaging brand experiences will be "gamified." The promise of gamification is that ordinary, even boring tasks can be made fun, engaging, and competitive through game mechanics and techniques. Gamification will creep into many aspects of everyday life, including shopping, education, entertainment, and wellness regimens.

There was a wonderful post on www.hideandseek.net in 2010 entitled, "Can't Play, Won't Play."[3] In this post, Margaret Robertson talked about how the gamification trend was really a misnomer. She insightfully renamed it "pointsification." Many activities today, especially commercially influenced activities such as working out at the local gym or saving money at a bank, are being pointsified. Participants can earn points and recognition badges for their activities. The gist of the critique is that games are inherently fun, interesting, and engaging, building on accumulated levels of skill. Games are played for their own sake, and points aren't the objective. On the other hand, points and badges can be effective reward tools for, say, educators. In other words, points systems are a valid way to motivate behavior, but perhaps using these systems is not really the same thing as playing a "game."

I agree that many commercial programs that will be called gamified will actually be pointsified. However, either way, I believe that this deep engagement with individual shoppers represents a welcome sea change from brand interactions of the past.

8. Context Creates Relevancy

Consumers who are immersed in digital contexts are usually at least somewhat emotionally and intellectually engaged. These contexts can be anything from shopping on eBay or at Macy's, to playing a game like Angry Birds, to writing on a friend's Facebook Wall. The environmental context includes in-game experiences, the embedding of one's social graph, an in-store experience, an in-home experience, or even simply wandering around the world using a filter like augmented reality. Content that enhances any of these experiences is relevant to the user.

Consumers value assets in virtual contexts more highly than what those assets may be worth in a "real-world" context. It may seem irrational that a virtual tattoo may be worth more to a Second Life denizen than that tattoo's "real-world" worth. However, the difference between the objective exchange rate (against fiat money) and the object's value in the digital context is the measure of the object's emotional value to the user. The value of branded virtual goods is elastic.

> The difference between the objective exchange rate (against fiat money) and an object's value in the digital context is the measure of the object's emotional value to the user.

Viximo's "Branded Virtual Goods Market Report" cites a perfect case in point. The report showed that a branded virtual good, Snoop Dogg's (virtual) hoodie, sold at a 345 percent premium over a generic hoodie, expressed in virtual currency. The emotional value of the brand to the players of the game was measured by this premium. Premiums for virtual goods are another way to extract value from shopper behaviors.

"A Branded Virtual Good can cost as little as $50 to create—and decreases to zero after designing the first unit of any virtual item. In fact, with the user effectively paying the brand for interacting with it, the overall CPM cost to the brand is negligible, if not negative—a compelling economic argument for brands that are used to paying $3 or higher CPMs for other forms of online marketing activity. Also, while costs decrease, sales—driven by viral behavior across the social graph—increase. This buzz-inspired growth, when combined with essentially infinite online shelf space (i.e., server capacity) and no real inventory management issues or costs, plus the benefits of new users coming into these communities continuously, creates a powerful and profitable scenario for real world brands. Finally, while virtual goods' gross margins of over 90 percent may seem like a good enough return on investment, the ability of virtual items to drive real world product sales is growing and may potentially be the greatest prize of all."[4]

9. "Tracking Kills Transparency"—Larry Lieberman

Moving forward, real financial returns may be determined on a shopper-by-shopper basis, because shopper behaviors (including purchase) can be tracked longitudinally. As companies like Buddy Media, SocialVibe, and others ramp up and refine their tracking tools, marketers will be able to offer each shopper financially appropriate incentives in real time. Imagine that a brand (in real time, at the point of sale) could potentially bargain with shoppers concerning future commitments or other collateral.

Tracking shoppers, which includes prospects as well as buyers, will be the goal of many a marketer in the next few years. While this may seem to be a daunting task, marketers may not be swimming upstream in this effort, as consumers are becoming inured to exchanging information for convenience or customized value.

Unless regulation inhibits this dynamic, many prospects and buyers will be captured in a kind of *digital census* of shopping, sharing, and buying activity. To some extent, they already are. The amounts of data derived from opt-in programs are pretty small compared to the massive data exhaust left by so many shoppers as they surf, browse, chat, and search. Right now, Google, Facebook, and Amazon have the best access to these data. According to the *Economist*, "The company that gets the most out of its data is Google. Creating new economic value from unthinkably large amounts of information is its lifeblood. . . . Google exploits information that is a by-product of user interactions, or data exhaust, which is automatically recycled to improve the service or create an entirely new product."[5]

Mining the data exhaust is a profitable endeavor, and often a competitive edge, for Internet companies. While these data are guarded, portions of these data may be sold to brands, and indeed already are, albeit in a limited way.

Even under these conditions, there will always be a good percentage of consumers who are "missing in action," from the marketer's perspective. For this group of shadow shoppers, good old segmentation and transparency techniques will come into play.

In the near future, we'll see more real-time, individual tracking data in the marketer's toolset. At a point in the more distant future, exchanges of value for participation, attention, advocacy, and loyalty will in part be determined by algorithms and artificial intelligence marketing programs.

10. Marketers Need to Think in Terms of Optimizing Investment in a Basket of Shopper Behaviors, Beyond Purchase

Too often, participation, loyalty, and advocacy are afterthoughts bolted onto a marketing program or brand idea. These behavioral objectives and metrics need to be fully built into a marketing proposition and the financial benchmarking of success. Shopper behaviors have financial value, and this can enhance brand value, not only by increasing conversion, but also by creating some insulation from competitors.

New tools like those at Buddy Media and SocialVibe will emerge to help shopper marketers entrench these objectives—both strategic and financial—into marketing plans, alongside more traditional goals like purchase and penetration.

Advocacy

When shoppers advocate for brands, it is earned media. The success of these programs can be measured by the number of shares, reshares, and other buzz metrics. Fortunately, these can be measured directly, along with the resulting sales. Sales conversion from shares and reshares is a measure of success akin to coupon redemption levels. It may become possible to create advocacy incentives unique to each shopper, based on the reach and effectiveness of her efforts.

In terms of strategic advantage, shopper advocacy has been shown to be as much as twice as effective as paid advertising. If the advocacy program builds a well-defined and desirable group of cohorts, then a strategic advantage may be gained over competitors too.

Participation

Participation is another form of earned media. However, this is interesting because the shopper is promoting the brand to herself, in a kind of auto-promotion. He is gaining compensation for participating in brand activities that embed him in the brand, building a hurdle to his engaging with competing brands. Because participation programs are opt-in activities, transaction anonymity can be eliminated for these shoppers even before they are at the point of sale.

Participation can be measured by the number of participants (and the desirability of their profiles), traffic driven to a store or event, and any resulting buzz.

Attention

From a marketing perspective, compensating shoppers for their attention is another form of paid media. Shoppers are rewarded directly with fiat currency, virtual currency, scrip, or charitable donations. These expenditures could be a portion of the total paid media budget, against a narrower target. (If softer forms of compensation are offered, such as entertainment or information, then the model is closer to traditional paid advertising.)

Strategically speaking, in-game ads and other context-relevant communications can boost the effectiveness of the message among a pinpointed group of buyers. Increasingly, interactive advertising blurs the line between attention and participation.

Loyalty

Generally, it is less expensive to keep a customer than to acquire a customer. A loyalty program is worthwhile when the retention cost is less than the customer lifetime value. The increasing sophistication of algorithms may mean that brands can bargain with shoppers for the value of future sales, based in part on their data exhaust and sales history.

To stay competitive, brands need to plan for shopper currency value exchanges financially, strategically, and logistically.

Finally, of course shopper behavior does not fall neatly into four categories. However, by designating these categories of shopper currencies, I hope to establish an approach that marketers can use to leverage the conscious value exchanges that shoppers are making every day.

CHAPTER 11 Recap: *Marketing Implications for the Near Term*

1. Shopper behaviors, beyond purchase, represent strategic and financial value to marketers.
   - Behavior that can be exchanged for value is shopper currency.
   - There are four primary categories of shopper currency: attention, participation, loyalty, and advocacy.
2. Shoppers are marketers' new pay-for-performance vehicles.
   - Shoppers' social graphs will be ubiquitous and accessible.
3. The age of the personal endorsement deal is upon us.
4. Advocates are not necessarily the same as heavy buyers; each should be marketed to differently.
5. Virtual currency will be increasingly frictionless and fungible with fiat currencies.
6. More brands will own both primary and secondary markets for their goods; that is, they will own the whole product life cycle, including reuse, and will provide incentives for buyback programs.
7. Gamification will creep into many aspects of everyday life, including shopping, education, entertainment, and wellness regimens.
8. Context drives relevancy, increasing the perceived value of rewards.
9. Tracking kills transparency.
   - When marketers can track attention, participation, advocacy, and purchase longitudinally, real financial returns can be determined.
10. Marketers need to think in terms of optimizing a basket of shopper behaviors, beyond purchase.
    - Brands need to plan for this value exchange, both strategically and financially.

12

A Glimpse Ahead

> "An analysis of the history of technology shows that techno-
> logical change is exponential, contrary to the common-sense
> 'intuitive linear' view. So we won't experience 100 years of
> progress in the 21st century—it will be more like 20,000
> years of progress (at today's rate). . . . There's even exponential
> growth in the rate of exponential growth. Within a few decades,
> machine intelligence will surpass human intelligence."
>
> —*Ray Kurzweil*, The Age of Spiritual Machines, *1999*

THE RATE OF CHANGE IS ACCELERATING

Even if one doesn't subscribe to Kurzweil's notion of the Singularity, it is hard to deny that the rate of change (both technological and social) is increasing. Therefore, this discussion of change and trends doesn't end with the immediate implications, but looks ahead to possibilities that may result from those changes.

Toward this end, I interviewed Walker Smith, executive chairman of the Futures Company (http://www.yankelovich.com/).

During our conversation, he outlined four major themes, which I have commented on here.

1. The Internet of objects will become bigger and more important than the Internet of people. It will shape our living environment, our choices, and the way we make decisions. The devices of the future will be packed with applications.

The changes that are occurring today will be shaping our lifestyles in the future. As the Internet of objects overtakes person-to-person communication, the stage will be set for an increased dependence on devices for decision making, and perhaps for other activities such as security, logistics, and personal care. Supplying these kinds of services will require very refined programming and algorithms. Artificial intelligence (AI) may come to the fore, in a very personal way.

2. As streams of data proliferate, we will see more [business] competition by algorithm.

Consumers and devices are leaving behind enormous streams of data in the form of data exhaust. Mining this information will be the key to success for many firms in the future. The MIT/Stanford Venture Lab (VLab) described the phenomenon this way:

> "The internet and social media create a mountain of random, unstructured, and at times ephemeral data by-products, which may appear to be trash. Yet, one person's trash is another's treasure. . . . With each of these Internet exchanges traces of information, or Data Exhaust, are left behind. When correlated or

combined, these snippets can provide insight into political views, professional achievements, purchasing behaviors, and demographic information—pinpointing trend setters and leading indicators. Brilliant innovators now re-purpose this data stream, aggregating and analyzing the data to provide new products or services."[1]

This has also been referred to as "big data." Analyzing the big data will be less daunting than it may seem, as computing power will be accelerating alongside the generation of data. Data exhaust can lead the way to understanding how contagion, especially social contagion, occurs. Furthermore, analysis of data patterns can also help researchers create algorithms to predict social and economic events, like a political revolution or a stock market crash.

Predictive modeling based on vast stores of information may become quite refined and could guide strategic business and marketing decisions in deep ways.

3. What causes social contagion? Marketers are 50 years late to the party.

From a marketing perspective, understanding the phenomenon of social contagion is important to the future of influence. If the "key influencers" model isn't an accurate paradigm of social contagion, then the way marketers seed messages may need to shift dramatically. Sophisticated algorithms—that learn over time—may be the new mechanism for spreading brand communications.

4. Future conditions may drive the thrift economy, including activities like renting and barter. In the next several years, nontransactional exchanges will become important, but not dominant.

Walker Smith, of the Futures Company, stated that product ownership will become less important, with swapping and renting coming to the fore. Ken Nisch offered a similar perspective, suggesting that retailers will want to own more of the secondary market as a way of maintaining their profitability.

INTERVIEW WITH J. WALKER SMITH, EXECUTIVE CHAIRMAN, THE FUTURES COMPANY

September 16, 2011

J. Walker Smith is executive chairman of the Futures Company, a global foresight and futures research consultancy that is part of the Kantar Group of WPP. Walker has been described by *Fortune* magazine as "one of America's leading analysts on consumer trends," and he consults with clients globally about trends, futures, and business strategy. He is the coauthor of four highly regarded books, a columnist on marketing strategy for *Marketing Management*, a blogger on baby boomers for the Huffington Post, and a former weekly radio commentator for a public radio show about cities and community life. Walker holds a doctorate in mass communication from the University of North Carolina at Chapel Hill.

Q: What will be the most significant factors influencing the way we live and shop in the next five years?

A: *Technology will be the dominant factor in the next five years. It will be embedded in everything we own—it's the "Internet of objects." The Internet of objects will become bigger and more important than the Internet of people. It will shape our living environment and our choices in the marketplace. The devices of the future will be packed with applications.*

That is the single biggest factor; everything else is secondary. Of course, demographics are changing. It will be an older marketplace, in which aging boomers are more predominant. The economy is the big elephant in the living room. We may see a relatively slow-growth future. A slowly increasing GDP won't forgive all our sins, and the new world economic order will challenge us (although that latter influencer may be overblown).

So, technology will be the dominant factor moving forward. Increasingly, it will be part of the infrastructure of life. Machines will be sensing and monitoring the data stream around them, and this will change the way we interact with the world. The data that are available will be more vast and sophisticated than what we have today. The cognitive biases we have will be remedied, and our basis for decision making will change.

In fact, to a certain extent, this is already going on. The cofounder of WIRED magazine, Kevin Kelly, writes extensively about "personal informatics." (See Kevin Kelly's blog, The Quantified Self.²) Self-tracking is starting to take hold. People are using self-trackers to improve their daily wellness routines, carbon footprints, and so forth. Data streams will be gathered and analyzed using passive sensors. FIT codes are already a decade old. They are a transitional technology—they are part of the trend feeding into the Internet of objects.

Q: What will be the impact of gamification on American society? What sectors will feel its influence, and how deeply?

A: *Gamification is a faddish thing. It is an interesting way to describe the push to enhance the experience that consumers have in the marketplace. It is one of those marketing fads like the experience economy and creating customer delight. Companies engage in a mad rush to stay competitive, to keep the consumer experience interesting. In order to fight off commoditization, experiential differentiators will be increasingly important for branding.*

There is a whole group of people who are passionately addicted to gaming. The video-game generation and the one after it are a host of consumers who have a set of expectations concerning digital interaction. Marketers are trying to re-create that engagement around their brands, using gaming techniques. These methods, such as accumulating points and advancing levels of skill, are mostly used for loyalty programs and promotions.

We'll go through the embedding of gaming principles in the next five to ten years. Gamification loses its appeal if the games are all the same! The history of improving customer interaction is that pretty soon everyone has mastered the new techniques. The more we see of gamification, the less effective it will be.

We will discover new ways to interact with customers. This is the ever-evolving history of customer interaction. But good marketers are looking beyond this even now.

Q: What will be the impact of personal social capital on shopping?

A: *Recommendations from friends are more important than ever, first because companies have lost their credibility among consumers. But even without that, recommendations exert a disproportionate influence because of the noise of the media and the increasing savvy of consumers. People are smarter about parsing what advertisements are all about.*

Today, people are trying to embed themselves in a tighter circle of influence. You used to brag about how many people you'd "friended"; now you brag about the number of people you've "unfriended." People think of themselves as being in intimate circles of engagement for decisions they make in the marketplace.

The important question is, "What accounts for social contagion?" For many years, marketers have used a "tipping point"–type model of social influence. Klout is an attempt to identify the biggest influencers. But the highly connected advocates model is being challenged by social researcher Duncan Watts.³ Watts is showing that this old model of influence doesn't fit the data.

In the past, we haven't had the kind of social data that we have today. The old data gave rise to old conclusions. It is possible that we will discover a new model. For example, the level of personal receptivity is part of the question. Openness and receptivity are very important to spreading influence. How receptive we are will dictate which trends will emerge.

Klout itself is a bit amusing. The concept emerged as a contradiction of its premise. It measures the ability of people to create a phenomenon . . . that Klout didn't create!

This whole issue requires deeper study. From data, we know, and have known for a long time, that happiness and depression are demonstrably contagious. Marketers are just half a century late. How it works is the key question.

The data trails are being tracked, but we need to put them to use. Data are necessary, but not sufficient, to answer this question. The algorithms that are put to use make the difference. It's like a competition for who has the better algorithm. The database marketers, including car dealerships, catalog marketers, and others, have known this for years.

As the streams of data proliferate, we will see more competition by algorithm.

Q: What is your vision of the impact of convergence (all media) on in-home behaviors and shopping? Also, would you share your thoughts about peer-to-peer currencies and virtual currencies?

A: *In terms of shopping, media at point of sale is still a huge underdeveloped opportunity. The shopping experience has remained virtually unchanged for over a century. We have innovated within that environment, but we have not fundamentally changed it. Convergence can change that.*

In a simple example, the converging of video and social media has made a new environment for connections with consumers. In turn, we will get better at tracking people's interactions with converged media, and we will have more to analyze. We will understand those dynamics better than before.

A big issue here is that product ownership is losing its importance. We will see more swapping, stealing, bartering, and partial ownership models showing up. Consumers want to have the benefits of a product without owning it. In this context, virtual currency makes more sense, because a real product isn't being purchased.

Take for example, swapping clothes—you aren't swapping money. Those kinds of transactions involve value that is not carried by money. Future conditions may drive the thrift economy, including activities like renting and barter. In the next several years, nontransactional exchanges will become important, but not dominant.

MACRO ECONOMIC INFLUENCE ON SHOPPER VALUE EXCHANGES

To broaden my perspective on the future, I had a conversation with Chris Keating, economic trends consultant. Keating predicts that there will be slow growth in the next decade, and as a result, he sees increasing pressure for alternative forms of income. "Additional sources of purchasing power will become more important and can include things like virtual currencies." If Keating is right, this factor will be an accelerator of behavioral value exchanges, as outlined in *The Shopper Economy*. This could also result in retailers owning more of the secondary markets for goods.

Keating speculated about what conditions would be necessary and sufficient for a predominant virtual currency to develop. In order to work, the new currency would need to be agreed upon, like a Bretton Woods–type treaty, but the parties would be major players in etail, social media, and search. This model has some similarities to agreements among nations, but in this case the entities would be corporations, not citizenries. The marketplace is primarily digital, not geographic.

INTERVIEW WITH CHRIS KEATING, ECONOMIC TRENDS CONSULTANT

Keating Consulting specializes in qualitative consumer trend analysis for Fortune 500 companies and their agencies. Keating built the financial services practice at the consumer trends company Iconoculture. He has served as SVP and worldwide account director at Foote Cone & Belding (now Draftfcb). At FCB, Keating led all global branding, advertising, direct marketing, interactive, and promotional activities for Chase Manhattan Bank/JPMorgan Chase, and also global direct marketing for Citibank credit cards (30 countries). He was also a group account director for AT&T's Business Services division and Consumer Out-of-Home Services group.

Q: In your opinion, what will be the biggest factors affecting American lifestyles in the next five to ten years?

A: *The biggest factor is the housing market; it's not going to get better. It will be 20 years before we see improvement.*

There are a few reasons why this is important. Since the Depression, a basic consumer concept has been that your home is a solid middle-class investment. In most cases, this is also the consumer's biggest investment. But this concept has blown up. The consumer's psyche and perception of personal wealth have been negatively affected. People do not perceive themselves as wealthy anymore.

In the last few years, people couldn't migrate to where the work was because they couldn't sell their homes. High unemployment rates have also diminished the perception of personal wealth and security. This has been a very rough road, and as a result, people are exceedingly cautious.

From an economic standpoint, there has also been a real loss of income. In fact, during the peak of the boom, close to a trillion dollars a year, or about 10 percent of real income, was being extracted from home equity. Money was extracted to pay for college educations, home repairs, and other major expenses. This is real wealth drying up. It's been a body blow to the American consumer. Home equity was the second source of income for many, and it must be replaced by something else.

This brings us to the implication for the future of American lifestyles. Increasingly, there will be pressure for alternative forms of income. Additional sources of purchasing power will become more important, and this can include things like virtual currencies.

Next, media convergence will have a huge impact. And who knows what that may look like! Think of this: the smartphone was introduced only in January 2007, and since then there has been a stunning rate of change. We will see enormous productivity on a single device.

Ongoing convergence will continue to the degree that we are willing to give up privacy. The trade-off depends on the consumer, of course. From this perspective, we may see more quasi-Tea Party–type movements that focus on consumer-centric rights. The reason is that the collection and processing of data are resting in the hands of government and industry.

The third factor is macroeconomic. Access to health care and the price of that access will continue to be restricted. In particular, the pure demographic pressure of the boomers will be felt. Another five years of population from that generation will bring that much more pressure on the system. The needs of aging boomers will draw down resources.

This will dampen spending and access for all others. And again, the impact on spending power across the board will be negative.

Finally, we will be paying for everything more overtly. The downsizing of government will mean fewer services. This will disproportionately affect poor people. The incredible disparity between rich and poor will get worse and worse.

Q: In terms of currencies, how do you see the role of localized currency or virtual currency in relation to fiat currency?

A: *The thing about currency is that it's only worth what you perceive it to be worth. Of course, it can be anything from land or livestock to beads or coins. That's why people still want the gold standard; gold is inherently valuable. But as a rule, to the degree that there is trust, a currency works, and to the degree that there is disruption, it won't work.*

For this reason, the euro could break down. The notion of decentralization is strong—you can't have a bunch of different policies and one currency. If some countries defect, it could shake up one-third of the world's currency.

Localization of currency can drive local businesses, especially in times of disruption, but you would need an exchange marketplace. For example, if you own Ithaca dollars, that value would need to be translated into U.S. dollars. Otherwise, Ithaca dollars couldn't be used to buy airplane tickets and cars.

The exchange sites, such as Points.com, are interesting. But it's an issue of scale. They are super tiny. The legacy systems of fiat currencies dwarf them. Every second of every day, trillions of U.S. dollars get moved around the world. A localized currency would involve me and my friends or maybe my local community, but probably not a billion other people.

We have certainly seen that consumer movements can have revolutionary power. But top-down fiat has some advantages, especially in terms of infrastructure. Today the U.S. dollar is the de facto global currency—90 percent of international transactions rely on the dollar. Because the world operates on superstructure, it is difficult to see that a localized currency could displace this.

Q: Could a virtual currency be an alternative to fiat currency?

A: *With the exception of Bitcoins and a few peer-to-peer currencies, shopper-generated points are converted into fiat money. For example, grocery store points are earned by spending dollars, and Shopkicks are spent in terms of dollar value.*

So—that's the big dividing line. If you look at the origins of most shopper point systems, they can be traced to dollar values. They have their roots in the system. In order for a virtual currency to be a real alternative, it would need to meet a few requirements.

First, it would need to be more convenient than other currencies or better for commerce. Perhaps it would have more purchasing power than the other currency.

Next, it must be stable; it can't lose value. Recently, I saw that Bitcoin had had a bubble. This kind of volatility isn't beneficial to value or trust. It would also need some sort of centralized backing. Perhaps multinational companies could guarantee its worth in terms of merchandise and services. The currency would also need to be agreed upon. Just like the system developed at Bretton Woods after World War II, the currency would need to be the result of an agreement among powerful entities. This would mean that the currency would be accepted in many places for private and public debts, and it would be tradable and fungible.

This kind of currency could be imagined if it were backed by major global corporations. As a thought experiment, let's pretend that Google, Facebook, Amazon, Walmart, and Apple backed a single virtual currency. The companies would be required to accept the currency for payment, at the same agreed-upon values. The money couldn't suddenly lose value or acceptance. This would be the Bretton Woods of leading e-commerce companies. It would be a kind of coalition or consortium program. It might work in theory.

However, once these virtual currencies or activities became large enough, they would not be able to escape government scrutiny. Let's imagine that this system is creating value out of whole cloth, with its origins outside of the fiat system. If the transactions were no longer dollar-driven and the currency was driving commercial transactions of, say, a billion dollars a year or more, the Feds would grow very interested.

THOUGHTS FOR THE FUTURE OF THE SHOPPER ECONOMY

Changes in technology and society are unpredictable, but the trends we see today will lead to the world of the future. Tomorrow, shoppers may want or need help navigating a marketplace that is bursting with information and choices. This need could give rise to personal artificial intelligence (AI) "assistants," who could become quite embedded in the lives of their owners.

Imagine a personalized decision-support avatar that could help the user filter information and make well-informed decisions, in addition to representing that person to brands and people. This avatar would be present everywhere the owner designates, including social media, web TV, mobile devices, and other objects like cars, dishwashers, and point-of-sale checkouts. The advantage of owning such an assistant would be to get relief from the influx of information, decision points, and messages. People could program high or low levels of information exposure and customize all aspects.

Likewise, businesspeople, marketers, and brands may have sophisticated AI tools to optimize their participation in the marketplace. Both buyer and seller would rely more heavily on decision-support software tools, which in turn would talk. Here is one place where the Internet of objects is especially relevant for brand communications. In this scenario, marketing efforts would have algorithms that would advertise from the seller's machine to the buyer's machine (or from software program to software program). In this setting, marketers would need to include the ability to sell to avatar assistants as well as human shoppers. This is a possible direction for the shopper economy in the future.

While these intermediaries may seem like further separation of brand and user, in fact, I believe that they will lead to a much greater degree of intimacy with shoppers. The reason is that if shoppers begin to rely on AI software for decision support and representation, intimacy with brands can enhance their lives without intruding as coarsely as it does today. Shoppers would make fewer decisions, but they would have more control. They might make a single choice to have a deeper brand relationship that would be perfected over time, building a barrier to switching. And as buyers become increasingly embedded in the brand proposition itself, the dynamics of shopping will be forever changed.

CHAPTER 12 Recap: *A Glimpse Ahead*

■ The Internet of objects will become bigger and more important than the Internet of people. It will shape our living environment, our choices, and the way we make decisions. The
devices of the future will be packed with applications.

■ As the streams of data proliferate, we will see more competition by algorithm.

■ Future conditions may drive the thrift economy, including
activities like renting and barter.

■ Additional sources of purchasing power will become more
important and could include things like virtual currencies.

■ A personalized, decision-support avatar may help shoppers
filter information. Marketers would need to learn to sell to
the shopper's artificial intelligence avatar, in addition to the
shopper herself.

Notes

CHAPTER 1

1. Robert Borden, "How to Earn Free Cell Phone Minutes with Virgin Mobile's Sugar Mama Program" August 7, 2007. (Voices.yahoo.com)

2. In other countries, such as Japan, shoppers had scan capabilities on their mobiles years before American shoppers.

3. Phil Hoops, "Get a Kick out of Shopping with a New App," *South Orange Dispatch*, August 25, 2010.

4. Max Chafkin, "How to Get Customers on Facebook and Twitter," *INC.*, March 1, 2010; http://www.inc.com/magazine/20100301/how-to-get-customers-on-facebook-and-twitter.html.

5. Wendy Liebmann, "How America Shops from Buzz to Buy," WSL Strategic Retail, October 2010.

6. Ibid.

7. In many contexts, virtual currency means value that is redeemable only for virtual goods, such as an in-game enhancement. In this book, I use the term *virtual currency* to mean any digitized, redeemable value other than fiat currency.

CHAPTER 2

1. "Feel Like a Wallflower? Maybe It's Your Facebook Wall," *New York Times*, April 10, 2011.

2. BBC Technology, "Facebook Sorry Over Face Tagging Launch." BBC.co.uk, June 8, 2011.

3. Television is evolving to create seamless convergence with the Internet, including interfaces with personalized digital content and mobile devices. When convergence reaches critical mass, many successful advertisers will already have mastered talking to their customers as individuals in this format, as well as to distinct groups of friends and family. But as of this writing, television is still essentially a business-to-consumer mass format.

4. Don Peppers and Martha Rogers, *The One-to-One Future* (New York: Currency Doubleday, 1997).

5. Shopkick.com, June 12, 2011.

6. Amanda Lenhart, Rich Ling, Scott Campbell, and Kristen Purcell, *Teens and Mobile Phones*, Pew Internet & American Life Project, April 20, 2010.

7. "Game-based Marketing: Inspire Customer Loyalty Through Rewards, Challenges, and Contests," Gabe Zichermann and Joselin Linder, Wiley, March 2010.

8. Stephanie Strom, "Louisville Fights Obesity," *New York Times*, June 13, 2011.

9. Nancy Miller, "Manifesto for a New Age," *WIRED*, March 2007.

10. Honeydefender.com, June 13, 2011.

11. *McKinsey Quarterly*, April 2010. "A New Way to Measure Word-of-Mouth Marketing" Authors: Bughin, Doogan, and Vetvik.

12. Bailey review, "Companies Must Not Pay Children to Promote Products," *Telegraph*, June 3, 2011.

13. Source: couponingtodisney.com.

CHAPTER 3

1. Source: adage.com/century/icon.

2. Deloitte & Touche and GMA, "Shopper Marketing: Capturing a Shopper's Mind, Heart and Wallet." 2007

3. "P&G Pushes 'Store Back,'" *Shopper Marketing* magazine, March 1, 2010.

4. Jenny Liu, "The Zero Moment of Truth," Google CPG blog, March 29, 2010.

5. Finkel, P2PIP2PI, "Defining Shopper Marketing," P2PIP2PI.com, August 29, 2008.

CHAPTER 4

1. Gabe Zichermann and Christopher Cunningham, *Gamification by Design: Implementing Game Mechanics in Web and Mobile Apps* (Sebastopol, CA: O'Reilly Media, 2011), p.10.

2. Procter & Gamble, "Thank You, Mom. By P&G," Facebook, July 2010; http://www.facebook.com/thankyoumom?utm_source=eds&utm_medium=crm&utm_campaign=July11Newsletter&sk=app_125560890854531.

3. Varolo.com, August 2011; http://www.varolo.com/tour.php?villageName=xanadu.

4. Samira J. Simone, "As Recession Lingers, Coupon Use Jumps 27 Percent," CNN.com, January 29, 2010.

   Some 3.3 billion packaged goods coupons were redeemed in 2009 compared to the 2.6 billion redeemed in 2008, marking the first time in 17 years that consumers used more coupons than the year before, according to the study by Inmar, a North Carolina-based company that tracks coupons and promotion trends.

5. Ron Ruggless, "Restaurant Chains Check Out Foursquare to Check In with Customers," *Nation's Restaurant News*, August 11, 2010.

6. However, with the advent of digital tracking and exhaust data, it may be possible that sellers will track each individual buyer's share of requirements.

7. David Aaker, "Secrets of Social Media Revealed 50 Years Ago," HBR Blog Network, June 17, 2011.

8. "Earn Points," Mysears.com, July 2011; http://www.mysears.com /help#earn_points.

9. Cottonelle.com; https://fresh.cottonelle.com/Social.aspx.

10. Poise.com, July 2011.

11. Livingsocial.com; http://livingsocial.com/deals/70107-100-to-spend-on-photo-services.

12. Ravi Mehta, virtualgoodsinsider.com, June 23, 2009.

CHAPTER 5

1. The Net Promoter Score was first introduced by Reichheld in his article, "The One Number You Need to Grow," *Harvard Business Review*, December 2003, pp. 46–54. Reichheld expanded on these ideas in "The Microeconomics of Customer Relationships," *MIT Sloan Management Review*, Winter 2006.

2. Reichheld, "Microeconomics of Customer Relationships," p. 73.

3. Timothy L. Keiningham, Lerzan Aksoy, Bruce Cooil, and Tor Wallin Andreassen, "Linking Customer Loyalty to Growth," *MIT Sloan Management Review*, Summer 2008, pp. 51–57.

4. J. Bughin, J. Doogan, and O. Vetvik, "A New Way to Measure Word-of-Mouth Marketing," *McKinsey Quarterly*, April 2010.

5. V. Kumar, J. Andrew Petersen, and Robert Leone, "How Valuable Is Word of Mouth?" *Harvard Business Review*, October 2007.

6. P. Conroy and A. Narula, "A New Breed of Brand Advocates: Social Networking Redefines Consumer Engagement," Deloitte, 2010.

7. Source: buddymedia.com.

8. Klout.com, 2011; http://klout.com/corp/kscore.

9. Simon Sinek, *Start with Why: How Great Leaders Inspire Everyone to Take Action* (New York: Portfolio, 2009), Kindle edition, pp. 427–429.

10. "PepsiCo to Launch Social Vending Machine," Reuters, April 27, 2011.

11. Source: www.lululemon.com.

12. eMarketer, "Case Study: Snack Brand Doubles Facebook 'Likes' Through Social Coupon," August 16, 2011; http://www.emarketer.com/Article.aspx?R=1008543.

13. Carolee Sherwood, "Is It Bad to Buy Likers on Facebook? Not Necessarily," *Retail Customer Experience*, August 4, 2011; http://www.retailcustomerexperience.com/article/182953/Is-it-bad-to-buy-Likers-on-Facebook-Not-necessarily.

14. Source for cases and share/conversion facts: Buddy Media.

15. Slideshare.net, "Reaching the Social Customer: New Tools, New Strategies" (Buddy Media) November 29, 2011.

CHAPTER 6

1. Source: http://www.collectivebias.com, July 2011.

2. Jennifer Alsever, "Even Bad Reviews Boost Sales," *CNN Money*, September 28, 2009.

3. The Sims Social fan page, August 22, 2011.

4. Dunkin' Donuts Facebook Fan Page Wall, September 1, 2011.

5. Matt Holliday, "Branded Virtual Gifts on Facebook Pages Opening New Doors for Viral Advertising," Insidefacebook.com, April 21, 2009.

6. Source: http://content.socialtwist.com/case-studies/SaraLee-SocialTwist-CaseStudy.pdf, August 2011.

7. "Extreme World of Warcraft Powerleveling—Level 1–60 in 20 Minutes," moneyne.ws, September 9, 2008; http://moneyne.ws/2008/09/09/extreme-world-of-warcraft-powerleveling-level-1-60-in-20-minutes/.

CHAPTER 7

1. Source: spgpromos.com, July 2011.

2. "7-Eleven Zynga Promotion," Best Sponsorship or Tie-in Campaign/Best Use of Games, Contests and Sweepstakes, Promo Pro Awards 2011 Finalist, PromoMagazine.com, August 3, 2011.

3. Source: Prizelogic.com.

CHAPTER 8

1. Richard Thaler, "Mental Accounting and Consumer Choice" *Marketing Science Magazine*, Summer 1985, vol. 4 no. 3

2. Colloquy.com, *Censustalk* "The Billion Member March: The 2011 Colloquy Loyalty Census" April 2011, p. 2.

3. Source: greenpoints.com.

4. Om Malik, "Why I Love Foursquare," November 24, 2009; http://gigaom.com/2009/11/24/why-i-love-the-foursquare/.

5. Amie Ninh, "Study Reveals Most Mobile Users Aren't 'Checking In,'" *Techland*, May 5, 2011; http://techland.time.com/2011 /05/05/study-reveals-most-mobile-users-arent-checking-in/#ixzz 1SZOlUmxD.

6. Ibid.

7. Mary Madden, Susannah Fox, Aaron Smith, and Jessica Vitak, "Digital Footprints," Pew Internet & American Life Project, December 16, 2007.

8. Source: Google.com, July 2011.

9. Diamond Foods, Pop Camera Action! 2010, in conjunction with MARS Advertising; http://popcameraaction.com/.

10. Stephanie Reese, "US Social Gaming Revenue to Pass $1 Billion This Year," eMarketer.com, June 28, 2011.

11. Ibid.

12. Source: capitalone.com, July 2011.

13. Source: Spin.com, 2011.

14. http://www.youtube.com/watch?v=YbRx5CGCM50&feature =fvsr.

15. Emile H. L. Aarts and Stefano Marzano, *The New Everyday: Views on Ambient Intelligence* (Uitgeverij, 010 Publishers, 2003), p. 46.

16. http://www.google.com/mobile/goggles/#text.

17. B. Joseph Pine and James H. Gilmore, *The Experience Economy* (Boston: Harvard Business School Press, 1999), pp. 61–62.

18. Ibid, p. 68.

19. Tom Ryan, "NRF: Disney Realizes the Product Isn't Everything." RetailWire, January 14, 2011.

20. Rick Nash, "The CXO: Why the Time Is Now for Customer Experience Officers," RetailCustomerExperience.com, May 16, 2011.

21. Phil Izzo, "Nearly Half of Americans Are 'Financially Fragile,'" *Wall Street Journal*, May 11, 2011.

CHAPTER 9

1. Paypal.com, 2008.

2. J. Cigliano, M. Georgiadis, D. Pleasance, and S. Whalley, "The Price of Loyalty," *McKinsey Quarterly*, no. 4, 2000.

3. RetailWire.com, April 20, 2011.

4. Cigliano et al., "The Price of Loyalty."

5. RetailWire.com, April 20, 2011.

6. Ken Nisch, CEO, JGA, interviewed on shopperrevolution.com, 2010.

7. Jill McBride, "GameStop PowerUp Rewards and Best Buy Gamers Club Battle for Customer Loyalty," Spin Within Blog, June 2011; http://www.jzmcbride.com/blog/2011/06/gamestop-powerup-rewards-and-best-buy-gamers-club-battle-for-customer-loyalty/.

CHAPTER 10

1. Irina Slutsky, "Users Earn 'Credits' for Lots of Things, and Now for Watching Ads," *Ad Age* Digital, May 6, 2011.

2. Ibid.

3. Source: SocialVibe, 2011.

CHAPTER 11

1. James Wilcox, "Best Buy's 'Buy Back' Program: Not Such a Great Deal," *Consumer Reports*, February 10, 2011.

2. Emile H. L. Aaarts and Stefano Marzano, *The New Everyday: Views on Ambient Intelligence* (Rotterdam: 010 Publishers, 2003), p. 46.

3. Margaret Robertson, "Can't Play, Won't Play," HideandSeek.net, October 6, 2010; http://www.hideandseek.net/2010/10/06/cant-play-wont-play//.

4. Viximo, "Branded Virtual Goods Market Report," July 2010, p. 7; www.viximo.com.

5. "Clicking for Gold: How Internet Companies Profit from Data on the Web," *Economist*, February 25, 2010; http://www.economist.com/node/15557431.

CHAPTER 12

1. "Data Exhaust Alchemy: Turning the Web's Waste into Gold," MIT/Stanford Venture Lab, VLAB.org, January 2010; http://www.vlab.org/article.html?aid=304.

2. Kevin Kelly, "Personal Informatics," The Quantified Self.com, January 2010; http://personalinformatics.org/entries/kevin-kelly.

3. Duncan Watts, *Everything Is Obvious: Once You Know the Answer* (New York: Crown Business, 2011).

Index

About the Author

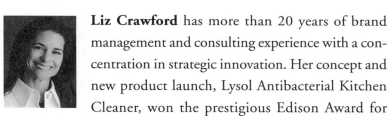

Liz Crawford has more than 20 years of brand management and consulting experience with a concentration in strategic innovation. Her concept and new product launch, Lysol Antibacterial Kitchen Cleaner, won the prestigious Edison Award for New Products. Over the last few years, Crawford has focused on developing integrated Shopper Marketing strategies for Fortune 500 clients. Her most recent staff assignment was senior vice president, Strategy for MARS Advertising. Currently, she is an analyst and contributing writer for the Path to Purchase Institute, publisher of *Shopper Marketing* magazine.

As a strategic planner and consultant, Crawford's clients have included: P&G, Safeway, Walgreens, Publix Supermarkets, Kraft, Pepsi, Nabisco, Johnson & Johnson, Coca-Cola, Kimberly Clark, American Greeting, Mars Candy, Hershey, Newell Rubbermaid, Y&R, BBDO, CIBA Vision, Spanx, and Pirelli Tires among others.

As a consultant and market researcher, Crawford has experience conducting focus groups in Europe, China, Japan, Morocco, Australia, and Mexico and throughout the United States, tapping into a wide array of demographic and psychographic segments.

Crawford has written feature articles for The HUB Magazine, CBS MarketWatch, and The National Review online. She is a member of RetailWire's BrainTrust Panel, and is also a regular contributor to the magazine. Crawford has been a featured speaker at IIR's Shopper Insights Conference Chicago, National Grocer's Association, American Marketing Association VA Beach, University of Chicago's Business Roundtable, Iconoculture's Iconosphere, and was also selected as the kick-off speaker at several corporate innovation off-site conferences.

She has been quoted as a marketing strategy and innovation expert in the *Associated Press, U.S. News & World Report, Barron's, ABC News,* the *Miami Herald, Brandweek,* the *Washington Times,* the *Sacramento Bee, Drug Store News,* and *New Products Magazine.*

She also taught as an adjunct marketing professor at Emory University's Goizueta Business School and New York University's Stern MBA program. She has an MBA from New York University and a BA in English from Barnard College, Columbia University.